ESCAPE
INTO REALITY

J. Hamilton Clarke

Escape Into Reality

J. Hamilton Clarke

Bag 6227
Fort St. John, B.C.
Canada, V1J 4H7

© 2000 John Hamilton Clarke

ISBN - 0-931221-43-9

**Ransom Press International
Bonita Springs, Florida**

Printed in Colombia

Table of Contents

Chapter 1	SEEDS OF FATE	7
Chapter 2	THE DAY SCHOOL BEGAN	13
Chapter 3	OUT OF THE ASHES	23
Chapter 4	BETWEEN DARK AND DAYLIGHT	33
Chapter 5	SPRING CAME ON A SPECIAL DAY	49
Chapter 6	YOUTH'S GENTLE AWAKENING	57
Chapter 7	THE SEVERED CORD	61
Chapter 8	CLIMBING TOWARDS SUCCESS	71
Chapter 9	THE GOOD YEARS	81
Chapter 10	SPRINGBOARD TO A DREAM	93
Chapter 11	ESCAPE	105
Chapter 12	INTO REALITY	121
Chapter 13	COUNTDOWN	139
Chapter 13	REALITY	147
Chapter 15	FREEDOM	161
Epilogue	FLIGHT	167

PROLOGUE

Exactly when the longing to flee from my roots began to take hold, I'm not sure. I do know it began at an early age. At first I wasn't aware that I was poor or that my life was obscure. I did not know that the mantle of insignificance had dropped on me at birth. True, the confinement of these disadvantages is a legacy inherited by many. However, not everyone learns of, or cares about, the barriers that separate them from the alluring, promising world beyond the walls of ignorance and inexperience. Only those who finally realise they are locked in a private prison discover inside themselves the desire to break out. Their need to escape is only as strong as the pain of the stifling, suffocating limitations the prisoner experiences. I slowly discovered my true condition and began to live with one purpose: I had to find a way out.

Some men and women experience the trauma of actually being locked behind penitentiary walls for crimes against society. They may dream of release or parole. A few even escape only to continue to be the same people they were before their imprisonment. Freedom to them, then, is a limited thing without wings. I wanted wings on my freedom. To this end I began to live, to truly escape from meaninglessness and from my own fantasies and dreams.

Ultimately, I did find the way out of my cell of inherited limitations, but almost simultaneously I came to question the terms of my accomplishment. To some, it would have been the pinnacle of achievement: I finally stood on the springboard to every dream a common man can hold. I was bathed in the golden light of youth, health and opportunity, but I didn't jump. Instead, I made my second escape just in time.

My story is two-fold; it tells of how I reached my golden moment and how I made a successful escape from it. This escape was not from stone walls or steel bars, but from a far more impenetrable prison – my own captivating success, achieved from the blueprints of my own dreams. Come with me across the span of years. I want to share with you the tale of my two escapes and how I found the keys to true freedom.

The earth, water and warmth of the sun are the eternal elements in the growth cycle; it's the seed that makes the difference in the harvest.

Genesis 1:11 (Moffatt)

God said, let the earth put out verdure, plants that bear seeds and trees yielding fruit of every kind, fruit with seed in it.

CHAPTER ONE

SEEDS OF FATE

I was birthed into a time warp of history. The "war to end all wars" had just terminated. After Versailles and the Armistice came peace. In the quiet countryside, south of Flat Head Lake in Montana, near a tiny village named after St. Ignatius, I arrived unannounced and unneeded into this life. The cold winds of the next to last day of January blew strongly that night. My arrival, fifth son in a hungry family of boys, brought small joy to my lonely mother. The nation had not yet recovered from the ravages of World War I, and was heading into the Great Depression of the '30's. The crash of 1929 would bring national disaster upon the heads of many, already desperate from long years of need. Mother, periodically abandoned by the father of her sons, staggered under the burden of our family's livelihood. My birth compounded her problems. In the years before welfare, social security, or the numerous benevolent social organizations we have today, there was simply no place to turn. The rules were simple: survive or die!

My father must be credited for the exceptional gifts he possessed. He had to be the world's greatest apologizer. As suddenly as he would disappear, he would reappear, unexpected, yet full of extraordinary accounts of his regrettable absences. I never became old enough to appreciate fully Father's skill in convincing Mother of his sincerity. He finally left, never to come back, a few years after my birth and before I could discover his secret. This I did learn: I was the result of one of his periods of apology. Two younger brothers were also products of Father's deep regret for his regular prolonged absences. I will not say I wasn't wanted, perhaps just not welcomed. Certainly, I wasn't needed. That tiny fault line of rejection for some becomes a crevasse. For me, it became a small mark upon the fabric that began to weave my character.

Father had a second unique ability. He could borrow money in a time when there was precious little to be borrowed.

He would approach the bank loan officer armed with purpose, promises, and persuasion. At face value and with only his signature, Father would leave the bank with a loan equal to his request.

With one of these magical loans, Father moved our family to Couer d'Alene, Idaho. We didn't actually reach the promising town on the lake's beautiful north shore. We moved to Cotton Wood Bay, then to East Point on the lake. We lived in these out-of-the-way places long enough for me to begin my memory bank. During this time period my next youngest brother, Monty, was born. Wayne, the last of seven sons, came a year or two later.

Three memories stay with me from our days at East Point. One was the old billy goat that chased me into a large stove sitting in our front yard. I was kept imprisoned for an hour in the stove's sooty interior before my yells brought my brothers with clubs to drive "Billy" away. The goat was from a herd that roamed freely about the Point. Once, we found him in our house, standing on the kitchen table, eating Mother's leftover hot cakes. Another time nearly cost the foul-smelling Billy his life. It seemed he was exploring our house one late morning hour and found his way to Father's bedroom through a series of open doors. It happened that my father was still in bed. Father awakened to find Billy straddling over him on top of the bed. The goat's musty beard hung in Father's face. Father came out of bed with a roar. The billy leaped off the bed and fled with his entourage of nannies and kids in hot pursuit, fleeing for their lives. Father could find neither gun nor bullets in time to do pesky Billy in.

My next remembrance is Mother's broken leg. The break was caused when a log she was skidding with our horse rolled unexpectedly against her leg and broke it. Looking back now, I realize Mother was doing a man's work. The logs to be cut into cord wood for the steam boats had to be skidded to the beach. This seemed to be the task Mother assigned herself. The broken leg slowed down Mother's skidding for a time. During her recuperation, Mother would take a row boat and fish on the lake directly past our dock. It was during one of these times my third memory occurred.

My older brother Harold must have been preparing the noon meal. My next older brother, Russell, and I were supposed to be helping. Water was needed. Russell and I were sent to the lake with small pails to obtain the liquid. Down the stairs we went, all one hundred fifty steps. Our instructions were clear – do not go out on to the deep end of the dock! Russell, known for his exact obedience, had filled his bucket near shore and was waiting for me to do the same. Even at an early age, I was interested in quality. If the water was good near shore, it would be much better further out on the dock. Ignoring my brother's warnings, I found a very promising place well out on the wooden dock to fill my bucket. There I reached far to get the very best water and fill my pail. No problem occurred until I tried to lift up my bucket full of excellent water. The pull of the bucket was too much. Losing my balance, but not wanting to let go of my prize pail, I toppled head first into the lake. I ended up in eight feet of water, standing on the lake bottom still holding my precious bucket. Rescue came when Russell's shriek for help was heard by Harold, who raced down the wood stairs at break-neck speed to pull me out. No, my past life didn't pass before me like a full-feature movie. My past life had been so brief, only a few frames would have been needed. I remember putting my free hand, not needed to hold my bucket, upward, then proceeding to swallow gulps of lake water. I became unconscious. Drowning does not take long. I believe I was nearly gone. I came to, feeling hands pushing against my chest. Mother was there now, having started rowing toward the dock at Russell's outcries. My father and oldest brother, Lewis, had also raced to the deck from where they were cutting cord wood on the beach. I'm sure I was both puny and obedient for a few days after my escape from a watery death. Years later, after another near death experience, I began to realize that an angel was guarding over my life. By now, I owe that angel a great deal of bonus overtime.

I think the billy must have gotten my father's goat! We moved shortly afterwards from East Point. I have puzzled for a lifetime as to Father's ability to migrate from state to state and area to area, making deals, loans, and moves – each move and change of location "more promising" than the last. Our small dairy farm, with its large barn and lanes lined with cherry trees, seemed promising. The farm lay only a few miles outside of scenic Couer d'Alene. The distant sound of mill whistles and the faint smell of coal smoke on frosty mornings, still lingers deep in my memory. Helping herd the cows along lush quiet roadsides, to return after idyllic sun-filled days, made those the happiest days of my young life. The home with its huge porch, bordered by lilacs and snowball shrubs was the nicest we had ever known. It was as if this particular expedition was intended to be the springboard of Father's last move with us all as a family.

Our peaceful, almost adequate days of food and comfort were numbered. The older boys had started school that year.

Suddenly, one day our tranquility was shattered. Father came home with the news that we were moving again. By now, moving was a routine. Father simply took what would fit the mode of transportation available and left everything else behind. My only treasure worth taking was a box of alphabet blocks – the first thing I was given that was truly my own. A kind neighbor had taken me with him to the town of Couer d'Alene. For me, this trip was extraordinary. Not only was it the occasion of receiving my first new personal possession, but also my first view of a town of any size. The experience was nearly overwhelming – such noise and activity. I didn't dare blink for fear of missing some rare enchanting sight. Alice in Wonderland had nothing on me for sheer excitement.

In contrast, our move to north central Washington is a total blank to me. Perhaps we traveled mostly at night. How Father found the next place we moved to is a total mystery. Like all his deals, this one had the same ingredients. A move to some out-of-the-way place, great possibilities, and a fly-by-night financial arrangement that could evaporate at a moment's notice. We arrived at a place called Republic, stopped for fuel, and wheeled on through town to a ranch on the road to Swan Lake. Twenty miles lay between us and the remote mining and logging town of Republic. Life on our timber-surrounded ranch, with its vast meadow and clear silver stream, began in late summer. Our hardships did not begin that winter. Father pulled a trick out of his magic hat, and became game warden and deputy sheriff.

Mother's recollections set the count of such actions at an even dozen, before wanderlust and total lack of responsibility took Father away from his family the final time. We learned later that a two thousand acre wheat ranch in Canada was also under consideration at the time of our move to Republic. Had the choice been different, I might have become a well-heeled Alberta wheat rancher. Had we moved to the lands north of the boarder at that actual time, a multitude of events would have been different.

No danger! With Father's skill of picking the most unpredictable situation, none of the above took place. (However, much later a thread of events did see me move my family to nearby beautiful British Columbia, Canada.)

The next summer the fragile thread holding a rocky marriage together finally broke. Mother must have made it final. No further apologies were accepted. Father departed for the last time.

Two things happened while we lived in the large log house in the forest by meadows. We suffered extreme hardships helplessly. Food was extremely scarce, money absolutely nonexistent. Mother reverted to back-breaking hard labor. She accepted a contract to cut railroad ties. Where she found the offer, or how it turned out, I don't know. One thing for sure, the Great Depression of the '30's caught Mother and us boys in its bear-like hug, and didn't release us for several long years. However, a monumental thing happened to me the second year of our move to Republic – I began school. That traumatic life-changing event comes back to me in graphic detail.

To nurture a life small and tender takes kindness woven with wisdom and understanding.

Proverbs 10:13 (KJV)

In the lips of him that hath understanding wisdom is found.

CHAPTER TWO

THE DAY SCHOOL BEGAN

The aroma of homemade biscuits that pulled me slowly from my comfortable cocoon of sleep into what would be a very long day for me. Mother's baking powder biscuits were matchless for sheer eating delight. I knew that oatmeal mush would soon be on the table and I would not be so foolish as to arrive late. I followed my next oldest brother down the steep stairway and nearly beat him to my place at the breakfast table. Large for his age, and older of course, Neal already had the large corner biscuit, first prize of mother's wonder breakfast, secure on his plate. Lewis and Harold, also older than me, sat with relaxed detachment across from each other near the head of the table, with the large pot of steaming oatmeal between them. Each, of course, also had a nice corner biscuit on his plate. I finally obtained a tattered biscuit of my own and some oatmeal. I made a small vow that some day, when I was grown up, I would eat only corner biscuits. I might even invent some way to cook all biscuits as corners. My attention was now diverted onto my portion of oatmeal. Before three fully-loaded spoonfuls arrived at my mouth, the early morning tranquility was shattered. Mother uttered only one word – School!

No other single word would change my life so totally. My mother standing tall, slender, and crowned with flowing dark hair, seemed to glance understandingly at me. I was not too young for school. In fact, I was well past my sixth birthday. This day could not be avoided. To me the word school ranked with the word Mars, a strange world far removed, for which I had had no preparation, no visits to school, no introduction to homework brought back by my older brothers. There had been no talk of schooling or what to expect. I now wonder if any of my brothers had attended school the previous year.

It was true that we had moved to this ranch with its mountain-encircled meadows nearly two years ago. My father had been with us part of the first year and had left in late summer. That winter had been long and difficult for mother and the older boys. We, the younger boys, were sheltered from that hardship by the incubator of extreme youth. I was comfortably tucked in age between the youngest at the time and my next older brother, Russell. I was past being a burden to anyone. Understanding the power structure of four older brothers and how to manipulate it, Russell seemed bent to my wishes. If I could only persuade one of the others, I could always hope to accomplish my desires.

Much of my life during the idyllic years before school didn't depend on concessions from my older brothers. I lived in a grand world all my own, simple and uncomplicated. Early morning warmth through spring and summer would draw me at daylight to wonders that could be enjoyed only in the first fleeting hours of each day, like the song of birds, strong, clear and urgent, signalling their calls for mates, food, and rights of domain. The cool quiet of the first morning would not be enjoyed long. Soon the bees, the magpies calling raucously, even toads and crickets, would compete with dashing butterflies for attention as the day raced into full activity. The meadow would also empty of the deer families finishing their feeding at its safe edges. One might be lucky to see them slip like silent shadows to sanctuaries known only to them. To miss such beginnings was to miss treasured parts of life.

Of course, each day held much more than the splendor of its first hours. After breakfast and minimal chores, the real business of each day's adventure began in earnest. The rich scent of catnip would lead me unerringly to emerald green beds with millions of blossoms to greet me. The snappy sting of nettles kept me alert to careless misjudgment. The great log bridge over which the road led to Swan Lake was many things to me. It could be a cave, castle, hideout, or a city by the sea as the need arose. I was a friend to the chipmunks and grey squirrels, even the frogs, whose favorite haunts I knew. Birds were also my friends. They told me secrets about where their nests were. They taught me early morning songs. Only the brook trout would not let me intrude into their lair beneath the overlapping creek banks. A flash of rainbow color, and once in a while a splash, was my reward for disturbing their peace.

Equal to the singing brook with its log bridge as a special place in my heart, were the trees. The truly virgin forest, far from sawmills, stood primeval as it had for multitudes of years. Only forest fire or extreme old age were enemy to these huge giants. As I would stand on the needle-carpeted forest floor, staring upward, my sight leaped from limb to limb until at last my view would burst out into clear blue sky above the tree tops. One was halfway to heaven by then! There were, of course, wonderful trees for climbing, each with its own treasury of foliage and secret recesses among thick branches.

Mother's voice brought me back to the day at hand. "John, you need to do something with your hair before you go." Using less than comb or brush seemed inadequate to Mother. A blast of breath shot from my lungs upward, past my nose, caught my brown shock of hair and swept it backwards out of my eyes. Then with a backward jerk of my head and the swift motion of my left palm, the wavy mass settled briefly in place before it would fall forward over my forehead again.

Five five-pound lunch pails sat in a row on our worn oilcloth tabletop – each with its tight-fitting lid and sturdy bail, the interior filled with biscuits and carrots. Mother's instructions were simple. "As you walk through the woods, stay together. Be quiet when you get into Mr. McDonald's car and wait for each other after school. You must come home together. Don't miss Mr. McDonald; it's too far to walk."

Two miles along the main road must be covered by eight A.M., so we headed out at a brisk walk. Walking was no problem for us. We walked everywhere. My brothers did not have to wait for me. I was strong and quick for my age and nearly the height of Russell, eighteen months my senior. I did not think about school on that two-mile walk. I did look back to see our log house slip out of sight as we were engulfed by great trees, and a sweeping bend in the road. It seemed to tell me it would be waiting when I returned.

Mr. McDonald was just coming out of his log house, followed by three children, as we brothers arrived in their front yard. I only had eyes for the remarkable shiny machine that sat there, more majestic than any other man-made thing I had ever seen. Only a giant silver Waltham watch held equal fascination to this beautiful 1929 four-door Model A Ford. We five boys quietly and reverently climbed into Mr. McDonald's Ford machine. I ended up sitting on someone's lap as eight children and a husky driver filled the green and black Ford to capacity. Out of the corner of my eye, I saw the curls of a girl's head and a snatch of gingham dress. I had not remembered seeing a girl up close before.

We were underway. The Ford motor seemed strong and powerful, its four cylinders sounding out their smooth rhythm. At the top of the panel called a dash was a most fascinating sight. A bubble of glass with cylinder-shaped marked balls inside bobbed and floated in some fluid. I had no idea as to its function, but it was marvelous to me. Beyond the windshield across the shiny green hood, sat the brass radiator cap gleaming in the morning sun streaming through occasional openings in the trees along our fairly smooth road. That brass radiator cap could serve as a crown, so purely grand it was!

By now we had crossed several log bridges that gave me just the briefest view of streams flowing beneath. There was no time to judge whether these would be worth exploring when I became big enough to venture far from home. However, none of the streams seemed to hold promise of being nearly as exceptional as our own creek at the ranch in the meadow.

Suddenly we crossed a different kind of bridge. It was smooth, made of even planks. The Ford picked up speed as we climbed a steeper place, leveled off, and stopped. We had arrived at a more main road than the one we had travelled for several miles. I could now see an automobile ahead of us going our same direction. A third was coming toward us. Mr. McDonald nearly could have reached out and touched it as it went past us on his side. I saw many houses, some of log and some made with smooth wood. It was impossible to see everything! Too many people, horses, houses, automobiles. I decided to look straight ahead and wait for "school" to appear. Mr. McDonald began slowing down his Model A. Then he stopped. We must be "at school." "All of you be here at this stop at four o'clock sharp," our driver told us. "Don't be late! We need to be home by dark."

The McDonald children said good-bye to their father and began running toward a large building with lots of windows. Lewis, Harold, and Neal walked slowly toward the far end of the building where older children were gathering. Closer to Russell and me, children of our own age were running back and forth yelling to each other. I could make no sense of their game, if they were playing one.

A woman appeared among the smaller children near the doorway and rang a bell in her hand. As we stood watching, the school yard began to empty. Children ran and quickly lined up near the doorway and marched inside. Russell and I were left standing only a few feet from where we had climbed out of Mr. McDonald's Ford. We looked at each other and began walking slowly toward the door everyone else had entered, our bare feet leaving draggy tracks in the soft sand of the school yard.

Suddenly the woman who had rung the bell came out again. She walked quickly toward us, asking questions as she came. She was younger than Mother, shorter and with a look on her face I had never encountered before. "Who are you boys? How old are you? What are your names and why are you late?" Before Russell could answer she said, "Never mind, we will find all this out." I'm not sure I could have said my name at that point. Children watched through the open window as we were led into the building. We followed the teacher toward the nearest room and took seats. She waved us toward the back of the room. As we sank into the seats, a couple of girls nearby snickered and the boy in the next seat whispered, "You're new here, ain't chu? I'll teach you how to fight at recess." Did the boy mean what Russell and I did sometimes, try to take each other down? Recess, what could that be? Fight? Did the boy mean.... I would learn many things. Some more quickly than others.

In the front of the room the teacher was talking while making marks on the blackboard. None of what she said made sense to me. Her voice seemed loud, but by the time her words reached me in the back of the room, I simply could not hear what she said. I knew my ears often ached at night and would sometimes drain on my pillow, but I did not know until after starting school that my hearing was impaired. On that first day I understood nothing of what was being explained by the teacher in the front of the room. I had neither pencil nor paper or book that first day. I sat locked into semi-deafness on the back row trying to understand what school was all about.

The day continued with more mumbled and jumbled doings at the front of the room. Our teacher's voice that began like quiet thunder faded away before it reached my desk. We had one more recess at which time I was introduced to giggling gingham-clad girls. I may not have learned anything in the classroom, but these little instructors were more capable at their trade than the mumbling teacher at the front of the room. They had found out my name and knew that I was greener than the grass growing along the creek at our ranch. Three girls with their bright eyes and decisive ways decided to do something about my further submersion into the quicksands of ignorance. These strange, alluring creatures waited for me outside of the school door. Like a barge on a lake I was towed away to be subjected to I knew not what. I soon found out.

In an area off the main runway, we arrived at what appeared to be a large square on the ground with small stones. I quickly learned that this was another school; the girls were the teachers and I the lone student. By now there were five frilly-dressed, intense, chattering girls around me, each presenting something connected in their minds with school. I was placed in one of the stone-lined squares and told to be quiet. The chatter increased, most of it near my ears. The girls shouted out words, numbers and non-decipherable things. Five minutes of this was all I could take. My nervous system was much overworked. My effort to get up and walk away was rebuffed, and about this time the boy who had promised to teach me to fight reappeared. He was set upon by three girls like bluejays after a cat trying to reach their nest. The other two girls kept me under carefully guarded house arrest. A small sense of panic gripped me. This was so new. The girls exhibited determination I had never encountered. It was easy to see that if I were to escape I'd have to make a break and run for it – something I could do well. My breakout didn't work in the flawless way I had planned. As I bolted out of the side of this fictitious schoolhouse, the little stones scattered in every direction. All five girls were directly in my way and two had a good grip on me. The others formed a barrier to my escape route. I managed to break one girl's grip on my wrist with a reverse leverage that always worked on my brother. How we all ended up on the ground in a tangle, I'm not sure. Shocked cries and tears followed. In the next instant, out of nowhere appeared Teacher. Some of the girls, with dust still on them, huddled by her side. The look on Teacher's face seemed firmer than before. "John Clarke, you should be ashamed of yourself." I wasn't sure what I should be ashamed of. Maybe girls fought by different rules. Anyway, to sit in the schoolhouse all day and then come out at recess to play school some more, didn't make sense to me. I spent the rest of recess in my back seat alone, aware of two things for sure: the teacher was a totally authoritative force to be reckoned with, and girls would challenge all my resources to understand them and get along.

As school ended the boy who sat next to me said he would wait for me outside. As I pushed the door open and burst into afternoon sunlight, the boy who promised to teach me to fight came around the building and headed toward me. "Hey, new kid, I'm gonna show you something! His eyes were cold, like animals I've seen caught. I sized him up and saw he was bigger than me. My only hope was to run for it. I could see there was no friendliness in his movements; he intended to hurt me. By instinct, I pretended to go back into school, as the mean looking kid lunged toward the door to block my escape. Then I darted the other way and was moving at great speed around the corner of the school building, and toward my brothers and Mr. McDonald's Ford. Jesse Owens would have been proud of my burst of speed. The bully was not far behind. As I dashed in among my brothers, my pursuer tried to put on the brakes, too late! My older brothers, grasping the situation, caught him who had intimidated me all day, lifted him off the ground and shook him good. Then they gave him a long toss into the sandy school yard. The boy rolled a time or two and came up on his feet, running. He moved away with pretty good speed himself. Lewis yelled a warning he would not forget. "You touch our brother again, you'll wish you hadn't."

We were on our way home from the place called school. I hoped I'd never have to go there again, yet in some deep way

I knew I must. Only after Mr. McDonald's Ford crossed the smooth bridge and two log bridges did I relax a little. I had been sitting stiff on my brother's knees looking straight ahead. If anyone said anything to me, I'm sure I didn't answer. There was numbness in my chest. The next thing I knew, we were at Mr. McDonald's and getting out of his automobile. "You boys better hurry," the driver said, "it will be dark before long."

    Five boys like stair steps with five empty pails headed towards home and our meadow with its silver stream. We crossed one bridge with only two to go. A small crashing sound was heard in the underbrush to the right of us. Lewis whispered, "Stay close, keep moving!" As we reached the next to last bridge a mile from home, Lewis put his hand up and we all stopped. Five sets of eyes and ears strained. We were all rewarded by the sound of a quiet thud and splash as a wild animal leaped the creek only a few yards into the dusky underbrush. "It's old 'Coug,'" Lewis breathed. We all knew what this meant. A cougar, too old to hunt well anymore, had been on the prowl lately. A woman neighbor had been mauled, but not killed, a few days earlier. The news had come to our place by a cattleman riding horseback three days before. Lewis next whispered strange instructions. "Each one grab a rock." Were we going to throw rocks at old cougar? This was not what my older brother had in mind. "When I tell you, bang the rock on your lunch pail, yell, and start running!" No one needed further instructions. At Lewis' signal, we all began to bang, yell, and run. How long it took us to go the remaining distance, I'll never know, but I do remember I was not two yards behind when we raced out of the forest and arrived winded in our front yard. Mother and my youngest brother were out front to see what all the yelling was about. What happened to the cougar? I think he had to be more frightened than we were; no Indian attack sounded worse.

    I told Mother very little about my day at school. I looked at her face a few times that evening to be sure I was right when I felt Teacher's face had a strange look about it. There was no time to go outside even to the big corral where I loved to sit on the top rail and watch the moon come up. Of course, tonight the hungry cougar was out there somewhere, and no one went out. I lay on my stomach in front of the stove and studied the flickering light dancing with the shadows of deepening night around our living room. The day's events faded some and my pent up feeling receded. Being quiet helped. At mother's word I slowly climbed the steep stairs. By light from the kerosene lamp already lit in our long bedroom in the loft, I undressed and slipped into bed. A slight wind sang a low song in the branches of the giant evergreen just outside the window. My brothers were also getting into bed, but I hoped the light would burn for a while longer. I wasn't sure I wanted to be alone with my thoughts in the darkness. The light was still shining a few minutes later when the wind carried the distinct cry of the mountain cougar into our bedroom. I knew all my brothers heard that cry just as I had. I snuggled deeper under the quilt Mother had made for my bed, and before my eyes closed on the day school had begun for me, one last thought ran through my mind. Old Coug may be hungry out there tonight, but tomorrow he won't have to go to school! He can just lay high on a hill overlooking a green and quiet valley and study its peaceful stream. At least he'll be free somewhere deep in the forest to rest until morning. Then the sun will come up, the sky will turn blue and....

After fire, flood or volcano, just wait a time: something strong and beautiful will grow up out of the ashes.

Isaiah 43:2 (KJV)

When thou passest through the water, I will be with thee; and through the rivers, they shall not overflow thee. When thou walkest through the fire, thou shall not be burned; neither shall the flame kindle upon thee.

CHAPTER THREE

OUT OF THE ASHES

Old Coug may well have lived out the rest of his life in the deep forest, along pure streams, in hidden mountain places. We Clarkes didn't find as easy a sanctuary. We moved from the log house with its hardships to a valley where apples grew – where times might be better. At this point in our roller coaster lives, it seemed destiny entered and began to exert lifelong changes for us all. For me personally, the first tiny crack in the door of my obscurity occurred. For sure, we would continue to know want and loss for a good while yet.

The Okanagan Valley in the early 1930's was a refuge for part of the migration fleeing westward from the dust bowl. The valley was a land of apple trees growing along a river running south. The river flowed from the Canadian border through the Okanagan, continuing on till it emptied itself into the broad Columbia at a place called Patares. The Okanagan River was not long, but it was the life line of our apple growing northern Washington valley. The power-producing Columbia makes its way further south and west, past Portland, Oregon, out to the great Pacific. At Omak, where we settled, the valley spread out toward hills and mountains beyond. Mostly the fertile fruit-growing belt was barely a ribbon in width. To this day, the upper Okanagan lies secluded in north central Washington, far removed from cities of any size.

The house mother found for us was an unpainted, tinder-dry, frame structure. We may well have been that dilapidated dwelling's only occupants for some length of time. We were definitely its last. Our stay in its rustic interior wasn't long. Fire evicted us one warm summer day.

Russell, now duly appointed chief cook, was preparing a meal. The beans and biscuits were not cooking fast enough to satisfy Russell Clarke's desire. Help was needed speed things up. Coal oil, used in our lamps, was selected to give the kitchen stove a needed boost. That cup full of kerosene tossed into the old cooking range, not only heated up the beans and biscuits, but also the whole house as well. The rusted stove pipe could not contain the sheet of flame that shot upward. Fumes and sparks escaped into the attic to ignite the dry wood. The smoke of the blaze was first seen by a neighbor before we boys were aware our house was on fire. Some of our lives may have been saved by the same neighbor who ran two hundred yards through a plowed field to warn us. We were completely unaware that our house was burning in the attic and roof above our heads. The house burned completely to the ground. Mother, who had found a small paying job, came home that night to a pile of hot ashes and smoking embers. The dry tinder box of a house had burned so quickly, we survived with only the clothing on our backs. Lewis did save Mother's sewing machine and her prize geraniums. His right hand carries scars from glass cuts received in breaking the front windows to get the geraniums. The memories of that huge mountain of flames marked my young mind for many years. Often, a glowing cherry red sunset would trigger the fright of our family's tragic moment of loss. We had just arrived in the poverty-stricken valley with very little to our names. Now we possessed absolutely nothing! No doubt the loss of that fire trap house was providential. Had the blaze happened at night, some of our lives could have been lost in the infernal roaring in the darkness.

Greater in significance however, was a far more remarkable event. Mother found, as a result of the fire, two things. First, she gained a friendship with a man named Willus – the same who ran to warn us boys of the fire. Secondly, Mother found faith in God. Friendship with a man is one thing. A friendship with God, this was completely new and different! For all of us, this evening was of eternal consequence. So, faith followed the fire.

As darkness came that fateful night, our family was scattered. We all ended up in three different homes with neighbors who truly felt sympathy for the tall lonesome-looking woman with her handful of boys. Two older brothers went together to one home, the younger three with Mother to the rescuer's parents who lived on an apple orchard overlooking a lake a few miles from the scene of the fire and the extra to a third neighbor nearby. That night I laid on a bed made on the floor beneath a great clock that ticked and chimed throughout the long night. Every time I closed my eyes, I could see the great furnace of fire, red and glaring, blending with the lowering afternoon sun and sweeping from the earth all of our few worldly possessions. In fact, that scene would reappear many times without warning in a most disquieting way in the years to come. Morning finally came and a new day. A huge farm breakfast of hotcakes, eggs, bacon and plenty of milk fortified us all for the necessary and exciting exploring ahead of us. As quiet conversation regarding our future began even before the dishes were cleaned, we boys were dismissed to begin our adventures in exploring. Limitations were set. "Do's" and "don'ts" were outlined and we were released. Should we go first to the barn, see the animals, race through the orchard, or see the lake? No good plan was ever agreed upon. We raced in one direction and then another with no immediate danger of exhausting the possibilities. That night I did sleep! The clock didn't seem to tick, nor its chimes ring, and the fire didn't blaze in my mind when my eyes snapped shut in instant sleep. The day of full-forced activity brought a near-instant healing to the awesome memory of the day.

Next, a most unexpected event occurred. Mother became lawful owner of a house in the small nearby town – some kind of final settlement involving father's last sight-unseen deal. We didn't have anything else but we did have a house, a nice house, all our very own. An exciting trip was taken to see the new house. What a wonderful development! There was lots of room, large trees, and a great back yard, complete with lilac bushes and even a grape arbor. And best of all, there was a lazy, slow-flowing river only a few blocks away that offered unlimited adventures.

A second thing happened that brought yet another change into all of our lives. We continued to stay with the wonderful old couple on the marvelous orchard for some time while the new house could be readied for our moving in. Furniture had to be acquired – nothing fancy, just the most basic housekeeping items. Isn't it strange one cannot remember well how such things are accomplished? I'm sure many people gave us their belongings, some things were borrowed, and we did without everything else.

On a Sunday before we moved into our new home, our kind benefactors invited Mother to attend their church. As it all turned out, we arrived at the church for the evening service. I can't remember where the clothing came from that we dressed in for that visit to yet another church. But I do well remember arriving outside a store front building in the large touring car that night, and when the engine was shut off, the swelling sounds of singing came rolling out of the building – words to songs I had never heard before, sung with fervor I had never witnessed before. "What a fellowship, what a joy divine, leaning on the everlasting arms," could clearly be heard not only by us but by anyone else for some distance away. The small building was crowded. Friendly people somehow made room for all of us. The singing went on, loudly and fervently, led by a most earnest young song leader. A man I knew at once to be the preacher beamed a great smile in our direction. I really wasn't sure what I thought about all of this. But it wasn't for me to decide anything. This was Mother's matter; I would trust her to know. That was just the way it was. I did think that this building certainly was awfully plain for a church; there was not one statue and certainly nothing that slightly resembled gold anywhere. The benches were plain and hard, not curved in the seat, not even a little bit. A grey-haired man just in front of us stopped his singing just long enough to utter a rather loud "Hallelujah!" Before I could rivet my full attention on him, a small woman on the other side of us literally shouted, "Praise the Lord!" I quickly checked my brothers and my mother to see what they must think. They were, it seemed to me, rather enjoying it all. Suddenly, the song service was over. Men came down the aisle with baskets to give people a chance to give money. The man I had guessed was the preacher told the people it was more blessed to give than to receive. This puzzled me considerably. We had nothing to give and certainly needed everything we could receive. Other things went on. The people, all at one time, turned to look fully in our direction. The preacher must have said something about us being new in the church. The kind old couple who had brought us beamed broadly. Mother looked a little pale. This had never happened to us before. We would all come in and go out of the churches we visited before with hardly any attention drawn to us at all. I wondered what caused the difference.

The preacher next declared his topic. Can a seven-year-old remember details of a sermon preached so long ago? I can still hear him say, "Agree quickly with thine adversary while you are in the way with him, lest suddenly he turn you over to the judge." I had very little understanding at the time about adversaries or judges, but none of this sounded good to me at all. The preacher was making it very clear that a person could be in real trouble if he didn't do something just right and soon. More admonition followed. It seemed for a long time that the preacher wasn't smiling anymore. Why had he become so serious? The next thing I remember, he was telling the people if they wanted to do the best thing, they should come up front and he would pray for them. He even asked people to raise their hand if they thought they needed help. I didn't see my mother raise her hand, but she must have. I was occupied watching others raise theirs. I noticed Mother crying about the time the preacher asked each one who raised their hand to come to the front of the building. To my great shock, Mother stepped into the aisle and started forward. This had never happened before. None of us boys were prepared for it. We looked at each other. Then one of my older brothers nodded toward the front. We all understood the signal at once. We were in this thing together. There was only one thing to do – follow Mother to the end of what she felt to do. We all got into the aisle and marched forward. Whatever Mother was doing was one thing. We only knew that whatever it was, we were going to back her all the way! And back her we did. When she knelt, so did we. She was weeping openly. We couldn't manage that, but we all stayed on our knees until she finished. Mother looked a very sorry sight. Her hair was messed up, her eyes swollen and red, and tears had done something awful to the front of her dress. The surprising thing that puzzled me was that she seemed happy about it all! Some of the ladies who had prayed rather loudly around her while she wept, now crowded around her hugging and saying, "Bless the Lord, Sister." Now the preacher came over to her. He was smiling again very broadly. His remark was, "God has been good to you, Sister. Jesus has just saved you." He asked all the people to praise the Lord because a new name had been written down in Glory!

An amazing thing happened next. The people began to sing a song with the very same words the preacher had just said. "There's a new name written down in glory and it's mine! Oh yes it's mine!" How could they do this? Just like that, make up a song and even a tune to it. I was greatly impressed. Before, all the songs came out of the book and had a page number. The preacher next looked very intently at all of us boys and said, "Isn't it wonderful when a whole family is swept into the Kingdom of Heaven." I was not sure what being swept into the Kingdom of Heaven meant, but I was sure it hadn't happened to me or my brother Russell. I did think something might have happened to a brother just above us two. Mother now began crying softly but her face was radiant. There was no question that she seemed very happy. Something had happened to her. She simply wasn't the same. Her countenance was different. The hungry look was gone. That faraway look was not there anymore. It seemed that the God she had looked for for so long had found her. Mother's search was over. She was satisfied. We visited very few other churches after this. From that day on, Mother always chose what we learned later was the Pentecostal church and that was her way for all the years that followed.

Mother took to the Pentecostal church like fish take to water and birds take to air. It consumed her whole life. Prayer seemed to take her over. Soon her nights seemed to be filled with prayer. She was first to the altar, last to leave. Now mother had much to pray about. No God-fearing woman with seven sons, who longed to see them follow her example, lacked things to pray about. Actually, I should have said six sons, because tragedy struck again. This time, the youngest, Wayne by name, age four, on a warm summer day, simply ate some wild flowers and in a few hours was gone to join his sister somewhere, wherever lonely little spirits meet.

When Mother no longer led us in her searching, the two oldest boys found jobs. They were gone more and more.

The day came when it was clear they must seek for themselves their way to go and the things to which they would hold. The schooling the older boys were to receive came to an end. But for we who were younger, the changing times held much more. Our schooling was only beginning in many ways. Like two ships running abreast in the open seas, Lewis and Harold's lives held very similar courses. Neal was next in age and for years his life ran parallel with Mother. We three who were younger followed similar paths to each other. No, it wasn't instant parting. Only slowly but surely, the drift began and the ships at sea found themselves far from each other. It was simple. Each was destined for a different port. This is not the story of what happened to all my brothers. That account is yet another chronicle. This account is really the continuing growth of my beckoning and call – a search birthed of something beyond me, something so strong and so drawing that I am still caught in its inexhaustible grip.

    Memories of the fearful fire slowly faded. Life in the long thin orchard covered valley became more tolerable. It would take World War II to extricate the little apple land from its prison of poverty. A small measure of my own personal liberation came with it. As a medium-sized boy of twelve, I obtained my first job for pay. Money was so rare in my young life, I never even dreamed of ever having any! The thirties were a grand time to have even a small measure of wealth. A small amount of hand cash could buy a dream.

    A twenty-five cent piece fell into my hands one day, absolutely out of the blue! No tycoon could have felt more sheer buying power than I did on that marvelous occasion. The valuable shining quarter lay waiting for me on the small busy main street of our town. Dozens, no doubt, passed it by. The coin had been lost somehow by someone to whom money was common – why were they not searching when I made my lucky discovery? Please realize that I came to no easy decision as to how to spend my fortunately gained booty. I have never been sure I spent the rare coin properly. Giving the money to Mother would have, of course, been the right thing to do. A small sack of flower, sugar, or even salt, who knows what else, could have been purchased. I did give money to Mother from my first job and funds earned for many years thereafter. The treasured quarter I kept and spent. At no time in my life have I ever felt more wealthy. My first purchase was a bandanna handkerchief, brilliant red and white, the ultimate possession. A tablet thick with lines was next, and two pencils each with its own eraser. The difference between the common penny pencils I had always used and my new beauties, was like the difference between a pony and a thoroughbred horse. Being wise and knowing that some day I would be reduced to penny pencils again, I bought with my vanishing wealth, a great eraser – one that, with care, would last a full year. Two final pennies bought a handful of jelly beans, and my splurge was over. Yes, I had to explain my sudden buying power. Some of my jelly beans helped pacify my envious older brother. Loans of my pencils, eraser, and sheets from my tablet gained me new friends. For days, my bandanna handkerchief never left my neck, day nor night.

My first job came to me from my best friend, Dick, who was my same age. His father, foreman for a wealthy orchardist named Mr. Ragsdale, created the job to introduce his son to profitable labor. Dick, who would be away for over a week, asked his father if I could take his place during his absence. The joy that filled me upon learning I could do the work carried me all the days of some very hard labor. My money-making task was to pull a 150 foot rubber spray hose for a man who sprayed the apple trees with an insect killing liquid. The hose was moved from spigot to spigot and could reach several rows of trees from the pipelines laid out through the orchard. The poison fluid flowing together was pumped from a central station where the insecticide mixture was made. Arsenic and lead, fish oil, and lime and sulfur were some of the sprays used. No one used the word toxic at the time. Twelve days later, and a dollar and twenty cents richer, I surrendered the job back to my friend Dick. For several years to come, I found employment with Mr. Ragsdale. Of course, as better times came, the per hour wage increased. My last work for Mr. Ragsdale years later, earned me the incredible sum of $1.25 per hour. The decades have passed like the shadows between sunset and dawn's brilliant displays. Pulling that long hose through head high sweet clover, leaving small bare footprints in muddy irrigation ditches, for ten cents an hour, started my slow crawl out of my grey chrysalis of poverty.

Harvest arrives in the Okanogan Valley and collides with mint fresh, crisp fall days. Reward for the whole year of labor, intensive and exacting, comes to the valley in a rush. One day, miles upon miles of fruit-laden apple orchards must be harvested. As apple prices improved during the 1940's, harvest time became the means by which families like ours, and migrants who came to the valley by the hundreds, made their winter stake. My winter shoes and coat depended on success in helping pick the red apples. Well, there were yellow and green apples also, but a crisp, huge, extra-fancy, juicy, Red Delicious has no rival in the world.

The J.C. Penney's store still stands on the same corner where mother bought our school clothes during those years long ago. We did have a large purchase of winter clothing stolen one fall by thieves whose crime equaled the Brinks robbery in scope of value stolen. Our family auto stood on the street full of our paid-for winter supplies unguarded for only a few minutes. The heartless robbers will never know the agony and broken hearts they caused by stealing our coats, shoes, underwear, and the pants that were to clothe us until the next fall. When a family is poor, like ours was, a simple disaster becomes a giant catastrophe! We did get by with handed-down clothing. Dick, my friend, gave me his old pair of shoes to wear and life went on. I went back to the same Penny's on that same Omak street corner not long ago, and bought some clothing. Somehow, there wasn't the same charged and choked feeling I felt as a child. Handing my visa card to the clerk didn't approximate the incredible accomplishment represented in handing over the very hard earned cash gained by exacting labor, picking those hundreds of boxes needed to gain only a few dollars.

I've always marveled at the powerful buoyancy of a life ruled by positive optimism – the sheer ability to work out of loss and tragedy with not much more than a backward glance. So was my childhood. There were many inbetween years, as I grew to youth and manhood. During those years, the joy of happy childhood helped me rise up out of the ashes and span a needed gap toward maturity.

Children are the architects of great dreams; playing them out brings the foot of the rainbow closer.

Ecclesiastes 11:9 (Moffatt)

Rejoice in your youth, young man, be blithe in the flower of your age; follow after your heart's desire and all that attracts you, but be sure of this, God will bring you to account....

CHAPTER FOUR

BETWEEN DARK AND DAYLIGHT

I pity the person whose childhood has been either nonexistent or tragically curtailed. One must have a full childhood in order to be paid fairly for entering into this sometimes harsh and seemingly unfair world. Actually, I wrestled a full and happy childhood from a time and conditions that intended to cheat me out of it all.

Poverty and a broken home is a good start to a strikeout. Take away a small boy's major role model, drag that youngster from place to place, disrupt his schooling causing poor grades, and you have the ingredients to create a troubled little soul. In my youth, the new kid at school was always rewarded with a sound beating or two. There were always bullies big enough to carry out this bloody ritual wherever our moves took us after I began school. It wasn't so much that I attended a great number of schools, it was the moving back and forth between the few I did attend, that caused the problem. Rarely able to start on opening day, I always found myself behind the class. A "B" class was created for students like me, usually made up of classmates who were discipline problems as well. I was saved from the "B" class by a warmhearted teacher, who heard a feeble plea out of a sensitive boy who found that special "B" classroom equal to a small scale hell on earth. To me that "B" stood for bad and bullies. Most of the students in that room didn't earn any grades. They would have to be considered exceptional in the reverse sense. Escaping from that fourth grade room, full of nine and ten-year-old hoodlums, may have been one of the major good fortunes of my childhood. My grades must have improved, because I was never threatened in that manner again.

Two other good things happened to me at this critical period in my growing up. Dick became my friend, and we moved to a house among apple trees, near a lake, in orchard country. Long clover-lined country lanes, sunflower covered hill sides, and the ever beckoning lake became a world friendly and safe. Dick and I became inseparable – not that I wasn't close to my nearest brothers. We simply had exhausted our bank of ideas. Dick seemed to open up a new dimension of enterprise and adventure. Dick's sister, Rachel, was a new intriguing consideration for me to fathom. My young life had no close encounters with girls. That whole world lay ahead of me. Rachel was to be a very slow and gentle introduction. There was much that must come first.

The sheer excitement of being alive, having a friend and all the world before us, made a place for me between the dark and daylight. This time was more than the children's hour the writer of the poem was describing. I entered into a grand journey through several years that filled my childhood cup to overflowing. I related perfectly to Huck Finn, Tom Sawyer, and Penrod. The expansive scale of their view of life, from the towers of their imagination, is something I must have matched at times. There were pirates, Vikings, and wild Indians at every turn. The landscape was at the same time the jungles of Africa, the Florida Everglades, and plains and mountains of the west. The world of Peter Pan, Robinson Crusoe, the Lone Ranger and Robin Hood blended together. Priority did rule however, so the launching of the battle cruiser, "Man of War" came first.

Dick and I labored long over the plans for this ship from whose deck we would rule the seven acre lake. Size became a factor we couldn't overrule. The materials to build the boat were at Dick's place. The lake was a mile and a half away. We were pleased that the construction moved along at a pace ahead of schedule. It soon became obvious, however, that our crew space would be very limited. Construction was discontinued when accessible materials ran out. It was time to drag the ship to the lake, christen, and launch it. Dragging the Man of War to water took nearly as long as building it. At the lake, Captain Dick made a fine christening speech. It was now time to launch our proud vessel. The several poles placed under and in front of the ship worked well, like a greased slide. The vessel gained momentum as it slid down the bank toward the lake surface. What a special moment! It was a moment for which we had worked long and hard. A very profound and totally unexpected thing happened as the "Man of War" struck the water. It simply continued bow first into the lake and within seconds disappeared beneath the waves. An enemy torpedo could not have done a better job. Our warship was sunk without a salvo being fired!

    Dick and I stood for some time staring in disbelief at the bubbles marking the watery grave of our hopes for a truly fine ship. What went wrong? Too much armament? As we walked up through the apple trees, now slightly bowed beneath their load of summer fruit, we began to discuss the possible construction of a motorized land vehicle. In my thoughts, a secret formed. I knew at once that this project would be launched, so to speak, at my place. I was in possession of the key component, a discarded but excellent old Maytag washing machine motor. The warm sense of coming success stayed with me after Dick departed for home to attend to belated chores.

    I planned to keep the secret of the motor for just the right moment. I must not fail to dramatize what a tremendous advanced implement we had at our disposal. I would watch for just the exact opportunity to tell Dick. Would he ever be surprised! Someone I must not tell was my younger brother, Monty. This would be a top secret affair. Younger brothers had a way of letting vital details be known that could jeopardize the most carefully laid plans – like the time Monty found the hiding place for my Lone Ranger outfit. He came marching in to the supper table wearing my mask. There was simply no way I would be able to roam the neighborhood totally unknown, behind my perfect disguise. I did tell the hutch full of rabbits some of the minor facts, as I fed them that night. I made sure no one else was within listening range.

    The vehicle Dick and I were going to build would excel, in looks and speed, the recent craft that won this year's national soap box derby! Her lines would be silky, I mean silky! Dick and I didn't begin on the secret project immediately. We got side-tracked by some good fortune. Russell, my older brother, was willing to join us for a considerably more urgent task – the building of a desperately needed fort. Forts, we could build very well. The one we constructed in Mr. Peterson's apple-packing shed was good. We removed certain boxes creating tunnels in the hundreds of apple boxes stored in this shed near our home. The war room was a sizable cavern in the very middle of the box pile. Tunnels led out in every direction to guard posts, and battle stations. We did end up with extra boxes that had to be stored elsewhere. We had abandoned this particular fort prior to the harvest when the owner of the storage building needed to use the boxes. I was told indirectly that some problems were encountered when the workers came to take the boxes out of the shed. It seems that the place and manner in which we stored the extra boxes not needed for our fort caused the men to use improper language. More improper language was used when the tunnels collapsed due to inadequate care by the men in dismantling the Fort Knox type installation. The big blow up came when the main war room collapsed in a great clatter and avalanche of the wooden boxes. It was mentioned that the owner wanted to talk to whoever had anything to do with "this mess" as he called it. I personally wasn't available, because my time was in priority demand working on plans for a new fort in an area some distance from the box pile complex.

The summer slipped by as easily as the white fleecy clouds high overhead. Happy days tumbled together like we boys did in the barn hay loft when the new alfalfa was brought in to be stored. Lazy hours swimming used generous portions of many days. The old moss-covered raft with its unsinkable logs continued to dominate the surface of the swimming hole.

We did dive to verify the resting place of "Man of War." On one such dive, I found something that propelled into me yet another pursuit that was to continue for a life time. Down some ten feet beneath the surface of the lake, almost hidden among the green growth, I caught view of something equal to buried treasure – a fishing pole, reel and all. I surfaced with my prize in great excitement. It was almost too good to be true. Who could have lost such a wonderful fishing pole? Surely they would be coming this very moment to claim their property. No owner showed up to claim the loss, and I began my fishing career. Nothing fills a young boy's life like the success of fishing. That collapsible steel rod with its sturdy reel and line often supplied a savory fish meal of lake perch for our family. I loved to swim with the fish, catch them, and eat them.

Dick was constantly staying overnight at my house. This enabled us to prolong either planning sessions or projects already underway. I did go to Dick's home, but not nearly as often. I didn't keep count as a child, but was well aware that there was a marked difference in the frequency of exchange of visits. Our house rested deep among the trees of our orchard. A path led nearly a quarter mile through the rows of heavily leafed sentries before breaking out into an open field two to three hundred yards from Dick's house. While our house was rather rambly, Dick's house was stiff and formal appearing. That stiff appearing house had once been the school building for the area. There was a great similarity between the houses and the families that inhabited them. Without question, our house was ruled by a laissez-faire system of loose schedule, meals at all hours, no bedtime, and fend for yourself otherwise.

While Dick loved the happy go lucky pace at our house, his house was ruled in quite a different manner! Dick's father was a most austere-looking man. Great bushy eye brows rested above dark piercing eyes. To me, he was a man to be avoided if possible, and when this couldn't be done, my rule was to be quiet and depart as soon as I could, gracefully. The Downey house was an ordered household. Perhaps the serious, sincere Brethren Church the family grew up in accounted for this. I'm sure the free-wheeling Pentecostal Church influenced our home in much the same way – causing a most notable difference in atmospheres of the two homes. Dick's family seemed to me to be much more prosperous than ours. Mr. Downey was foreman for an optometrist who owned a sizable fruit orchard. Actually, my step-father owned the orchard and acreage we lived on. Management was probably the chief difference. Apple prices coming out of the Great Depression were so low that only the most prudent growers made anything from their crops. The ever present coddling moths who became the destructive apple worms were not easily controlled. Don't mention early spring frosts, or scale, or hail in the summer, because if the grower survived all this, careless pickers could lower the quality drastically at the last moment. When I came to age and became aware of all this, I decided that Los Vegas gamblers had a far surer bet than the apple growers.

Wealth, of course, is a relative thing. I was seldom aware of any lack. Plenty of hand-me-down clothing from older brothers took care of my simple wardrobe. A new coat and pair of shoes for winter, and my needs were met. At least twice, Dick's discarded shoes became my school pair until apple harvest money came in. None of these facts of life pressed in on my young mind too heavily. The hazy glow of unconquered dreams swelled like a beautiful secret in my breast. This euphoric power carried me through the dark times of my childhood and deposited me into the broad daylight of youth and adulthood.

Many far more important things occupied my world of thoughts. Rachel was one of these delightful mysteries. I was greener than the grass that lined the irrigation ditches among the apple trees. A vacuum surrounded me concerning facts of life, or the world in general. I needed to learn everything worth knowing. The distinction between imagination and the real world came rudely from time to time. Mr. Downey was an agent of the imposed reality. Teachers at school and bullies on the school grounds helped me know about the real world beyond the safety zones of my summer and country sanctuary.

Dick and I slept one night outside on a warm summer evening near his house. A full moon kept us awake late and night sounds fired our imaginations and generated some stories to match. Finally, some crickets were successful in singing us to sleep. It seemed that the sun came up at once. Breakfast at the Downey table seemed like a ritual to me. I sat a bit spellbound at how everything happened. Mr. Downey sat a very imposing figure at the head of the table. Mrs. Downey and Rachel were bringing last-minute items to the table. I had never seen such ceremony. Dick's younger brother and another sister were seated along the table's sides while Dick and I had chairs at the end.

Just then, Mr. Downey looked my way, and his dark eyes rested upon me. I began to feel a claustrophobic closeness come upon me. "Hello, 'potty,'" Mr. Downey said to me, "what do you do for work these days?" "My name isn't potty," I murmured, "and I don't work yet, for money." The attention swung away from me as Rachel took her seat just beyond Dick. Mrs. Downey was seated, and the prayer began at the head of the table. This prayer was so solemn, I had no doubt that God heard the deeply intoned petition. The Pentecostal preachers could have learned a lot from how Mr. Downey prayed. I'm sure there must have been several things for breakfast that morning. I only saw one, the great box of shredded wheat. I watched intently while Mr. Downey withdrew his hand with a square straw-like substance and placed it in a bowl. I had never seen anything like this before. We had one cereal at home for breakfast always, oatmeal. Potatoes, eggs, and biscuits, often supplemented the oatmeal. But what was this new and amazing food? The picture on the side of the box was fascinating. It was of great waterfall like nothing I had ever seen. When I was given this small loaf of straw, I quietly waited and watched. Milk was poured over it and sugar added. Everyone began eating this substance with seeming delight. Somehow I wasn't hungry, but I was relieved when everyone else began eating. No one must see me steal a glance at Rachel. I did so with lightening speed. Brown eyes, brown long curls, and a face with the same deep tan tones as Dick's, caused by a summer in the sun, gave Rachel a Shirley Temple look. Rachel did look at me, with a glance I could not read. From that moment, I knew it would be a long time before I understood what all lay behind those big brown eyes.

Dick and I stood on the porch talking in the morning sun, before I left to walk across the field through the orchard, to my house. Just as I started down the first step, I felt a gentle but firm small hand push me sending me on my way. My full attention was needed to manage the next two steps, but I did turn in time to see Rachel disappear, curls and all, through the kitchen door.

I walked home through the open field and sheltering apple trees deep in thought. Why were things so serious in the Downey home? Why did Mr. Downey call me "Potty" when he knew my name was John? He seemed to grin inwardly at some humorous thought I couldn't understand. Then there was Rachel, a perfect question mark. She did push me, but not too hard. If my brother had done so, I would have sailed down the stairs and flattened on the ground. I concluded that I had a lot to learn and hardly knew where to begin.

I would not have to worry immediately about all the things I must learn. Summer was only midway through its pleasant journey. Everything could wait except one thing, the motorized land cruiser. On Dick's next visit I disclosed my secret, the Maytag motor. Dick didn't always show surprise, or great admiration for some of my ideas. This time was better than usual. "Do you think it will work?" he asked. It was the perfect question. Now was the time to dramatize my exceptional contribution to our new secret project! The small motor was well hidden behind a shed some safe distance from our house. I led Dick through the orchard, away from all prying eyes, before circling back to the cache under the shed roof. If only the thing would start easily! Slowly I pulled the wraps of off the motor. No oil or grime showed from its long years of use. I had carefully wiped it clean. Before Dick could respond, I stepped down briskly on the kick start pedal and the motor barked out its instant "put-put" answer. Dick stared in amazement as the cloud of blue exhaust smoke from the motor enveloped us. I quickly shorted out the coil and the popping sounds stopped. No one must hear us! "Man of War!" Dick exclaimed. "It's a beauty!" Dick's reaction was more than I could hope for. It was time to make plans and start construction on our silky, motorized land craft. Our plans looked good. My drawing was pretty good also, of course showing the smooth lines we hoped to duplicate in actual construction. Two things hindered us from accomplishing all we wanted to in constructing the vehicle – lack of tools and materials. The frame ended up a bit heavier and blunter than we wanted. Two-by-fours would certainly give lots of strength however. We collected four wheels that fit loosely onto the rods serving as front and rear axles. These were anchored to two more two-by-fours. It wasn't possible to keep the project secret after all. Our pounding and banging brought both Monty and Russell to see what we were doing. The big surprise of course, no one knew. This car would be powered! Russell came up with the idea of having the front axle swivel in order to steer the vehicle. It did make sense, once we realized that such a capability could save us from running off of the road. Apple boxes proved most valuable. Taken apart we had nails and material for a seat and front hood. Paint would have to wait, but a pulley we must find. A platform just ahead of the back wheels puzzled both Russell and Monty. "For cargo," I fibbed. No way were we going to let the secret out ahead of time! Now we had to come up with our best engineering! The rod holding the back wheels was placed inside a piece of pipe so it could turn. The pipe was wired to the back two-by-four cross piece forming part of the axle. We were getting close to our goal, but we needed a pulley that would fit onto the rod to match the pulley already on the Maytag motor. The gods smiled on us – we found a pulley that fit onto the rod. We wedged wood and nails in to make the pulley tight. All this was accomplished in secret. Russell and Monty lost interest when Dick and I seemed in no hurry to push the wheeled cart around. We would revive their interest all right, and that very soon when the test drive was made.

Late on the night before we planned to give a public showing of our silky motorized land cruiser, we set the motor in place. An old fan belt was just right to connect the pulleys on the axle and Maytag motor. We nailed the motor in place, making sure the belt was tight. Everything was ready for the public test drive. We went to bed excited over the promise of great success on the next day. Brothers Russell and Monty were on hand and even Mother stopped by on her way to the garden. Dick's younger brother, Clarence, came in on his bike, with a message about Dick being needed at home. So the time was ripe – everything was ready. We didn't name our land cruiser "Silky." That part just didn't happen. Maybe a better name would have been, "Tank." Our craft was wheeled out into broad daylight and I stepped in to ride away on our first trial. Dick stepped down on the kick-starter. Everyone stood expectantly watching. One of the advantages of our engineering was the direct drive arrangement of our vehicle; there was no clutch to wear out. Old gasoline and improper oil mix must have caused the great cloud of exhaust smoke when the Maytag motor started. As driver, I and the land craft were nearly concealed by a smoke screen. I still believe I felt a slight forward motion when the motor started. However, it stopped abruptly before the vehicle moved forward. The cloud of smoke slowly cleared away, revealing me and the land cruiser positioned exactly where we had started our test.

No one moved as I slowly dismounted from the square craft with its wheels sunk a good three inches into the sand. Mother spoke first. "How did you boys manage to get that old Maytag motor to run? I thought it gave up the ghost years ago." Monty wanted the next ride. Clarence warned Dick he was needed at home. Mother seemed about to leave. Only Russell maintained a relaxed detached interest. "Wait everyone, let's give it one more try," I shouted. "Quick, Dick, let's get it up on the gravel by the house." Everyone followed along – we still had our audience. "This time I won't ride," I explained, "we'll push it while we start the motor." Russell and Dick started pushing as I shoved down on the starter. A steady smoky "put-put" came from the back of the cart. "Let's go!" I ordered. Cheers rose from everyone as the empty cart moved on its own, creeping slowly down the graveled lane toward the main gate two hundred yards away. This unmanned "put-put" ran off into the alfalfa a few yards from the edge of the lane and the test was over. Mom went to the garden. Monty offered his services pushing. Russell suggested a larger motor. Dick got on with Clarence to bicycle home, and yelled over his shoulder, "Hey, John, how about using two Maytag motors?"

The next time I saw Rachel, Dick and I had gotten together to plan an expedition. The journey called for a heroic bicycle trip into particularly uncharted territory into the foot hills of the Cascades fifteen miles from home. Green Lake would be our camping spot. We would be armed with Dick's single shot .22. Our fishing poles would assure survival for this overnight saga. Minor details needed to be worked out like parental permission, supplies, and a borrowed bicycle for me. When Dick and I finished, Rachel gave me a half smile. I told Dick I should go home since I hadn't been there for hours. Suddenly, Rachel came close and tagged me on the arm. I turned toward her puzzled, only to see her run away. "Hey," I called, "why did you do that?" "Catch me and find out," I was told. Half-heartedly, I trotted in her direction. Zip! With curls flying, Rachel passed only a few inches from me going in the opposite direction. Wheeling about, I could see Dick standing on the porch grinning knowingly. It was clear to me that this was some kind of a game, but what were the rules? If I caught up with Rachel, what then? Within seconds, there was nothing to figure out. Rachel flew up the steps and disappeared into the kitchen. Without a goodbye, I did my own running, stopping only within the safe shelter of the apple trees. I went directly to feed my rabbits, knowing that girls were a total mystery to me.

The fall season came pleasantly. That crisp morning air began to carry away the dreamy warm summer lethargy. Harvest time and school opening were close at hand. There would be time for only one more major endeavor before our captivity began. School seemed terribly demanding, so regularly were there formidable powers to be reckoned with.

A major discovery set us to work on our final project of the summer. Indians! Large numbers were camping not far from where we must catch the bus for school. Dick reported the situation; there were many tepees, all set up on the far edge of a lake, near the large orchard tract owned by Mr. Peterson. We hadn't built our fort in time! Only extreme effort and good fortune could save the day. Dick, Russell, and I were out early the next day, scouting the situation from a concealment not far from the growing Indian encampment. "Look," I exclaimed, "right over there, material for our fort." Russell and Dick understood at once what I had in mind for the old car body completely stripped to the flat fire wall, and a pile of irrigation pipes. The Indians, a good hundred yards away, paid no attention as we began our fort. The car body was finally pushed, pried and propped into an upright position standing high in the air on the flat fire wall. Next came the eight-inch abandoned pipes. These were also stood upright around the rusty car body. Wire from more ancient wooden pipes bound everything together. Lunch was forgotten, and only the lowering afternoon sun alerted us to the fact that we had spent nearly a full day working on our fort. "Man of War," Dick exclaimed. "Isn't it a beauty!" Russell nodded and I agreed by declaring it was better than Fort Knox. We locked up and started for home. A quick plunge in the lake washed most of the dirt from us and our clothes. Getting home was now our priority, but we headed out knowing we were certainly more prepared than General Custer was for his Indian fight at "Little Bighorn." Our attack upon the circle of tepees would have to wait, since school would begin in two days.

School opening was a blur of emotions, sounds and smells – the smells of new shoes and clothing most of the other children were wearing. My old shoes would have to do. The tight feeling in my stomach always occurred as I was taken to a new room to meet a new teacher. Most of the students in my class were the same as the year before. "How do I always get to sit by Sadie? Why not by Jeanette at least just once?" The four mile bus ride had its own brand of noise. I didn't contribute any that first week. My share of noise making would come later.

On Friday afternoon, walking home from the bus corner, Russell, Dick, and I planned our attack on the Indians for the next day. Indians were everywhere. We noticed men picking in the apple orchards on both sides of the road home. We might just have them all leave, or take them prisoners – we'd see about that.

The route we took to arrive at our fort unnoticed went along by the shore of the large sister lake not far from our swimming hole. We slipped quietly in to the fort and secured our stronghold entrance. I climbed up to the look-out post and took command. There was only a little activity around the dozen or more tents, only a woman or two outside and some children. This whole thing would be accomplished in quick order. This would be no drawn-out battle! I checked to make sure Russell and Dick had their sling shots and rocks ready. "Bring plenty of rocks," I ordered. My two trusted lieutenants moved into their battle stations. This attack would be a total surprise to the unsuspecting Indians. "Fire!" I ordered. "Hit the high tent flaps." True to the mark, the rocks sailed away. Each of us chose a different tent. I was extremely pleased with our first shots. Right on target! "Select new tents," I ordered. Our aim was incredible. We could see the tent tops shake as the rocks zipped in. It was obvious the rocks banged down through the smoke vent hole and into the kettles and fire below. Breakfast for the Indians would be a bit delayed today! Before we could get our third shots away, women and children began swarming out of the tents. "I think this is it!" I cried. "They are going to surrender!" I was surprised to see no white flags. Instead, the Indian women came out with sticks in their hands and, like angry hornets, began running in our direction.

The first fist-sized rock thrown by one of the squaws shook our fort, raising a cloud of dust. I made a very rapid appraisal of our situation. If the women surrounded our fort, we were trapped. A small oversight left us without food or water. Then the full truth of our plight occurred to me. They might push our fort over. The Indian men might come. "Retreat!" I shouted, "every man for himself!" Dick was out first, and away in a remarkable burst of speed. I knew he was a good runner, but this was terrific! I came next, (so much for staying with a sinking ship!) By a last second burst of speed, I just barely slipped between two young Indian women and fled to safety. Russell was not so fortunate. I glanced over my shoulder just in time to see Russell run smack into a large-sized Indian squaw. Her arms closed around him and I knew my brother was a goner! I found Dick hidden in some thick willows. What will they do to Russell? We wondered. Bury him to his neck in the earth? Would he have to battle to the death with their strongest warriors? I really felt sad about my brother. He was very dear to me. Too bad I couldn't go rescue him.

We didn't have to wait long, before Russell could be heard muttering as he came near our hiding place. We could make out, "The dirty cowards, double-crossers!" What had the Indians done to him to make him feel this way. Russell was a mess. We learned to our surprise as we led him to the lake to clean him up, that Russell was talking about Dick and me. "They sat on me and gave me a pounding," Russell explained. "It was better that they not capture all of us," Dick argued. "We were just about to get a rescue party and save you." I took Russell's turn washing the dishes that night and he knew I was sorry for what the squaws had done to him. "Maybe we need three forts," I told my defeated comrades. "With tunnels joining them, we could surround the Indians." "At least we need to put the door on the back side of our fort next time," was Russell's suggestion. "That way we won't have to run right into them if we need to escape again."

The summer fled away in the same manner that we had escaped from the Indian squaws – in rapid order! In my fifth year at school I was introduced to three healthy influences that began to bring greater reality to my life – Stratton

Jane Porters's books, Sunday school, and non fiction reading. Mrs. Porter's books about Freckles and the Limberlost, written in the 1920's, were rich in the beauty of nature, hard work and integrity of character.

Mother's conversion to faith in God and His Divine Son, Jesus, carried us younger boys into church with her. At the same time, a wise school teacher introduced me to the section of books in the library about the true world of men, inventions, and discoveries and actual history. For the next several years, these nonfiction books made up the menu of my reading. More responsibility at home, and Sunday school training helped me paddle my canoe closer to the shores of responsible youth.

I did learn to play tag with Rachel. We finally were able to talk to each other without engaging in a game. Our friendship, formed in the sweet innocence of childhood, was like warmth without fire. About this time, I helped recover some things stolen from the Downey home. A sticky fingered boy who lived in the neighborhood had stolen some items, one belonging to Rachel. This action caused my stock to raise a little in Mr. Downey's eyes. Visits to see Dick and Rachel were a little more pleasant. Thereafter, my younger brother, Monty, was given the nick name, "Potty" by Mr. Downey.

The trip to Green Lake did materialize the next summer. Eventually, summer work in the orchards started for me. A new bicycle with a shock absorber on the goose neck was brought home by my older brother, Neal, and use of that bicycle gave a new dimension to the scope of my youthful freedom. Giving Rachel a ride on the front of that bike, her curls flowing in my face, was like gaining the heights of a new hill. Suddenly childhood was gone. Eighth grade graduation came and it was as if I found myself comfortably viewing a totally new vista of life.

Four chief angels watched over me during my between years. Russell was always there in steady loyalty. With Dick, there was exceptional trust, and deep comradeship. Rachel cast a gentle blanket of expectation over my life. Her untouched beauty and purity of soul became a symbol of a picture yet to be painted. My mother's prayers still ring in my ears from those years of recovery from hardship. Her faith, strong and fulfilling, is the same brand I have found refuge in all my days. My childhood was often sparse, but never empty. The simplicity of those years often calls to me when life becomes fast and hectic. Most of the indescribable dreams, all drawn then in faintest form, have come to pass. I simply walked out of the in-between shadow land of happy childhood, into the promising sunlight of youth.

Never should anyone live forever unless they were once fully seventeen!

Proverbs 4:18 (KJV)

The path of the just is as a shining light that shineth more and more unto the perfect day.

CHAPTER FIVE

SPRING CAME ON A SPECIAL DAY

Youth and springtime go together and one should take care not to ever lose either. I don't believe I ever have. Yes, brief winter times have come, and short stretches of summer heat, but always spring returns eternal.

It was the scent of apple blossoms that gently brushed back peaceful sleep on my most memorable spring day. Dawn's light gaining strength every moment, was perceptible through my closed eyelids. Not often could I afford an ordered wakening ritual – today I would. The contour of the canvas cot cradled my relaxed back a moment or two longer than usual before I slowly ordered my eyelids open. My ears, alerted to daybreak sounds, tuned in a distant meadowlark's morning song and a nearby robin's excitement at breakfast prospects. Every detail of my tiny tent cathedral came into focus. Soft shadows of overhanging tree branches and leaves moved slowly like mobiles on the slanted tent ceiling. Blossom petals left their faint outline before a gentle breeze would continue their flight to the orchard floor. Simplicity describes my canvas-walled tent chamber. Eight by ten feet is not a large interior, but for me it was spacious. In addition to the canvas cot, covered by a folded quilt pad and light blankets, a pillow and an apple box bedside stand completed the furnishings. That one cannot retain that quality of simplicity is a shame. Hunger for material things prevented me from doing so.

My body responded smoothly and without complaint as I placed my bare feet on the one luxury item of my tiny temporary private world – a two-by-four foot rug remnant appropriated by my chief gift, a glib tongue, from a source now long forgotten. Yellow cord trowsers, too new to be properly soiled, a simple shirt topped with my newly acquired "Omak

Pioneers" Letterman's sweater completed my attire for the day. I was ready to walk into the sunshine bathing the fully blossomed apple orchard. Saddle shoes would provide the smooth cushion for my glide through the day. Covers and pillow in place on the canvas cot, I slipped past the tent flap into the warm morning surrounding the tiny island of peace, where I would spend my nights for yet another month. Time would come for the green alfalfa to be cut, small apples thinned. My tent would then be moved to less busy surroundings.

The smell of hot cakes directed my nose toward the old house where we lived, barely visible through the trees. The moment I stood outside the small white tent on the carpet of deep green alfalfa, amid a shower of pale pink apple blossoms, was a moment of vibrant life. Every youthful sense was alive and fully aware. One word described how I viewed myself and the tiny corner of the world I knew anything about – PROMISE, covered with hope.

My growing up years were behind me. The struggle to maintain continuity in school attendance and at least average grades was won. Our family had not moved for nearly three years, allowing my first two high school years to be uninterrupted. Now my junior year was coming to a happy conclusion.

In January of that year, my sixteenth birthday came as had all my preceding birthdays without one candle, gift or remembrance. I expected none, so was never disappointed. On that day, I had arrived home early to a nearly empty house. A few moments later, my friend Dick came by, and casually suggested we take a short drive together. Dick had his driver's license and his father's Model A Ford. Our little country roads made their way mostly in squares, through the orchards now naked without their leaves. A few inches of snow mantled the open fields. Our talk of coming spring and summer and plans to someday escape our little valley held my attention until Dick suddenly turned into a driveway at the beginning of the four miles of oiled road leading to Omak, our home town.

"I need to give a message to the Kennedys," Dick told me, "It will only take a couple of minutes." As Dick parked and got out, he called, "Come along, you can say 'Hi.'" I knew the Kennedys; they attended the Pentecostal church I went to. They sometimes held youth meetings in their home. The snow crunched under my saddle shoes as I followed Dick toward the porch and front door. The early evening air was refreshing but cold. Lights were now on and shining through the windows. They looked warm and inviting. Mr. Kennedy responded to Dick's rap on the door. We were greeted with, "Come along fellows, don't stand out there in the cold." Mr. Kennedy led us from the small hallway toward the ample living room. Dick followed and I trailed behind. As we entered the living room, Mr. Kennedy stepped to his left, Dick stepped to the right. I found myself alone at the entrance of the room. The whole house seemed to explode with people. Several dozen came from every room converging upon me. "Happy Birthday, John Clarke!" rang in my ears for weeks. That birthday party with its candles, cake, gifts and games is now only a blur on my memory, but I have not forgotten the solid lift I felt in the index of my self worth scale.

For most of my sixteen years, I had felt accepted and included in my immediate family circle. Yes, Dick was a true friend, but the wide ring of closeness was mostly at church and a seeming few at high school.

Now months later as I hurried through chores and breakfast, making ready for the two mile walk to the bus corner, a small spark of excitement ignited somewhere deep within me. Today, the results of last Friday's student body elections would be made known. Each year, the officers were chosen by a party system. Any self-appointed group could form a party and put up a slate of candidates. I had always viewed the happenings with detachment. It never occurred to me that I would be involved in any way. Seniors formed the three or four parties, and juniors became the candidates. The slates of coming officers filled up and the political activities began. I was fascinated with the operations of a party directed by senior Ralph Barshers. Ralph, winner of a state and national oratorical contest, had selected a classical small town slate of candidates for President – Carol, Ralph's friend, whose father owned the town's historic James J. Hill Hotel; Jeannette, basketball cheer leader, a beautiful blond whose father was superintendent of the school district. The sects and treasurer slots were filled by the same quality prospects – young people of prominent city families.

Interesting events took place in the first week of the campaign. Two of the parties merged, combining their strongest candidates. It was obvious that Ralph and company were the team to beat. Next, the fourth party couldn't quite get their program together, lost heart, and dropped out. Excitement mounted. The few hundred members of the high school student body were infected by the mounting fever of amateur political activities. The whole matter would be resolved within two weeks, the time allotted for the elections.

On Friday of the first week, a special assembly was called, and candidates were to give speeches. The atmosphere was charged for two reasons. First, classes were going to let out early following the assembly, and second, rumors were about that big election news would be given at the assembly.

Jim McFarland spoke first as presidential candidate for the Reformed party. I always admired Jim. In my opinion, he was the smoothest fellow in our class. His speech and the resulting applause were great. Other members of Jim's party spoke, and Ralph's party was next. Instead of Carol, the presidential candidate, standing to speak Ralph himself went to the platform, turned and faced the student body. Everyone quieted down. Ralph had their attention. Ralph began, "Carol, this party's candidate for president, has come to a very difficult decision. She doesn't feel that she should run for the student body presidency as our candidate. Carol will come now and tell you why." I had thought the place was quiet before; now it felt like a tomb. Carol, taller than average and of regal appearance, came slowly to the podium. Carol was an excellent student and well liked. I couldn't imagine what had caused her to step down. We all soon found out.

Carol began, "Yes, I would love to have the honor and duty of being next year's student body president, and" she continued, "I believe I could have won over a very worthy opponent. I can assure you, I would have done my best if I had been elected. However, ever since I was chosen to lead our party, I have realized that there was someone else who should have the position." A buzz now went through the assembly hall. Like everyone else, I couldn't imagine who Carol might be talking about. I found out at the same time everyone else did. "There is one person more fully qualified, and able to do a better job than I can. I am hereby stepping down as candidate for president of the student body so that John Click Clarke can take my place."

Carol's last statement became our campaign slogan, "Let's click with Clarke." Ralph leaped back onto the platform and he, Carol, and their party's other candidates began to clap and call for "Click Clarke" to join them. The other students joined in. I've always had words to say, sometimes too many, but on that youthful day, I was overwhelmed. As I made my way forward, the thing that helped shape that day and many to come was the superintendent of schools, handshake. Mr. Morgan looked me directly in the eye and whispered into my ear, "You can do it John, get up there and prove it!"

Every life has at least one pivotal point. The election was secondary. To find out that I was appreciated and valued by that many teachers and students was without doubt, a key pivotal point in my life.

During the next week, I made speeches, another assembly or two was held, and election day came. I was not sure of the election at all. Actually, each candidate was on their own. The students were to vote for the person they thought would do the best job in that particular office. I really felt Jim would win and all my criteria backed up that thought. Jim lived in town, I lived in the country. The Pentecostal church I attended had a file of interesting stories that accumulated about things that went on there. Under oath, I might have had to agree that a few things were definitely different. Not learning to dance and not being seen at the movies or parties made my social life appear very flat.

Now, Monday and the day each candidate must reckon with had come – election results. We were summoned immediately after roll call to the Assembly Hall. I had hoped maybe the winner's names would just be written on the home room black board. Now, we'd all have to face the results fair and square. Names of winners were read in reverse. All office winners, except presidents, were read first. I looked at Mr. Morgan who was present for the election announcements. I wasn't sure, but he seemed to give me the smallest guarded wink. Mr. Perry, the high school principal, asked both Jim and me to come forward. "It was a close election," he stated. "You both did a great job campaigning. Either of you would have done a fine job. The one elected to serve next year's student body as president..." How could a man say so many words and not tell us what we all wanted to know? Then Perry announced, "The man elected to serve as the student body president next year is Click Clarke!" The clapping, cheering, and congratulations had a strange effect on me. I was sobered. From somewhere within, I realized that this honor would be followed by duty.

I did get through the next year. I received a lot of help. Mr. Morgan never knew what his talks meant to me. He would see me in the hall, and invite me into his office, which happened to be in the high school at the time. A quick tip thought or idea, and I'd be on my way. The classmates elected with me were of tremendous support. Ralph and Carol were most strongly committed to my success. Believe me, I even prayed a lot that senior year for guidance and help.

That marvelous spring day brought with it something far more important than the passing honor of being elected to that high school office. The new sense of value and self worth I gained that day began serving me. It's one thing to have the very essential family and friend support. The wider unexpected endorsement to my person and character was a much more global and lasting thing.

The small white tent set among the apple trees, covered with blossoms and sunshine, lies folded and forgotten. By now, the old brick high school building has been torn down and replaced by a new one. Ralph and Jeannette, two bright souls who played a key role in the election that year, are gone. They have departed this passing momentary scene. But that special spring day and its warmth, blossoms and triumph remain with me, unending to this present moment.

Awakening is much the same as the opening of buds, blooms and blossoms. The delicate sweet scent of promise is enough to cause one to wait for the fullness.

James 5:7 (KJV)

... The husbandman waiteth for the precious fruit of the earth and hath long patience for it ...

CHAPTER SIX

YOUTH'S GENTLE AWAKENING

One year later, another gentle warm day was ending delightfully with the sun sinking slowly toward the rim of the picturesque Cascade Mountains beyond our valley. The blossoms had set, the tiny apples had appeared, and Dick and I were working to thin the tender fruit. We had permission to stop work at five o'clock, an hour before our regular quitting time. By six we were bathed, dressed and halfway to our destination, a church youth gathering on the shores of beautiful Lake Osoyoos on the Canadian border about forty miles from home.

We had made this trip before. After we both had acquired the privilege of driving and earned our parents trust to use our families' precious vehicles, we had driven to an old fashioned camp meeting on the same lake. Held in a tent, it had been accompanied by lively music, singing and stirring Gospel preaching. Oh, we had listened all right, especially during the evangelist's altar call, for he made our young hearts turn sober and even quake a little. Hell seemed hot and heaven sweet, but we still found time to cast our eyes about a bit. We noticed some very attractive young ladies, a recent addition to our items of interest. Girls had always intrigued me, but they had nevertheless remained a profound mystery. Growing up with five brothers and no sisters had contributed to my ignorance on the girl subject. It was at that camp meeting the year before that I had first met Margie Widel.

We were again headed north to the lake but this time for a young people's meeting. We arrived safely in Dick's parents' newly-rebuilt classic Ford. The meeting remains a blur of events – singing, special music and preaching. But I clearly remember the sweet conclusion I experienced.

I didn't spot Margie until after the meeting and then with only a couple of protected glances to be sure she was there. I knew that she had just been chosen to represent her high school as its candidate for Apple Blossom Queen in the coming festival. Margie was "sweet sixteen" in more ways than one. Her direct, clear blue eyes that looked right at me made it hard for me to see her long, lovely dark brown hair or her tall, slender figure dressed in a plaid blouse and gabardine skirt. My seventeen years had not given me any experience that would have prepared me for that moment. My childhood friendship with Dick's sister, Rachel, had only served to cause my reverence and respect for girls to approach a certain level of near worship.

"Hello, John Clarke. Have you done any big game hunting lately?" Margie asked.

This was in reply to a letter I had written to her right after we had first met at that earlier camp meeting. I realized I might have overdone it a bit. Perhaps I had described too many exploits, including big game hunting, that could not all have been accommodated in the few years that I had lived. I hoped she wouldn't ask about my travels or some of the other things I might have mentioned in that letter.

Many of the smooth phrases I had rehearsed in my mind to say to Margie, should I ever get the chance, failed me now. Not one of them came to mind.

"Oh, no, nothing new, just work," I lamely answered.

But then I made a bold move and offered to take Margie home. This would only be possible if certain things worked out: If my brother Russell would ride back with Dick; if I could obtain permission from Margie's mother; if my mother, who had come earlier with my older brother Nea and his wife Mary, would give her permission; and if I could use our family vehicle, a well-used Plymouth of uncertain vintage.

Everything worked out wonderfully! Russell agreed (that was the easy part) to ride home with Dick. Margie's mother gave her permission for Margie to ride to her house with me. And my mother agreed to the plan as well!

First date. First love. First gentle awakening. The pure joy of such an innocent beginning, the splendor of such a moment! Why should it matter if Neal drove us in our family automobile with his wife by his side? What difference did it make if we took Margie's mother along and, oh yes, my mother as well?

When an experience is the first, it has no precedent to quarrel with; it is complete in itself. All I remember is being with Margie, fully satisfied with the sweet small beginning of the total enchantment of first love.

Oh, for the splendor of youth's gentle awakening, slow – innocent, beautiful... It was enough, just being near each other, young, alive, enjoying life's springtime!

Loose the warm clasp of parents' hands with fleeting backward glances to home and scenes familiar; ride the winds of change to places strange and distant. Gentle severing then takes place. At last the cord is broken.

Genesis 28:20-21 (KJV)

Jacob vowed a vow, saying, If God will be with me, and will keep me in this way that I go, and will give me bread to eat, and raiment to put on, so that I will come again to my father's house in peace; then shall the Lord be my God.

CHAPTER SEVEN

THE SEVERED CORD

Wars don't just happen, they are caused. When the unwritten history of the world is finally penned, it will include how World War II was caused. That chronicle will not include all the mountains of newsprint, radio broadcast and propaganda giving the reasons for World War II. The true record will show the true cause of war – the only cause for every war ever fought—greed, pride, and a struggle for power. Allowance will not be made to permit the inclusion of a growing number of zany, insane and totally dangerous and characterless people who have gained power in many countries. The plot plan and perpetration of that inculpable tragic deed, together with those who plotted it, will one day be known. A mere 20 years separated the two world wars. It was obvious something wasn't quite settled. The total cost of World Wars I and II will never be fully calculated – not in money spent or lives lost.

I was swept up into that second great conflagration like a dust particle pushed in front of the dust mop used by the janitor in our high school corridors. I stood in the Superintendent's office on December 7, 1941, and heard President Franklin Delane Roosevelt describe the day of infamy, the U.S. entrance into war with Japan. The Axis was formed. The mad rush to mobilize began like a freight train leaving the station. Within weeks, the draft, war bond rallies, victory core, and state guards filled all knowledge, space, and time. What would become the greatest war machine in history began to be built. I was a part of that U.S. war machine. A selective volunteer is one who volunteers before being drafted. I became a selective volunteer. My reward for doing so was to choose which branch of the military I would serve in. I chose the U.S. Navy medical corp.

A bus ride to Spokane for induction, a short trip to Farragut, Idaho, and I was on my way. Ties to life as I had known it would be cut completely and finally. That bus carried me away from parents, church, school, and the tiny sheltered world I knew anything about. A final physical examination by the Navy doctors nearly changed my above statement. A low-grade discharge was noticed in one of my ears. A loss of hearing was then detected, and I was given a choice: "You can be released for this condition," I was told, "because you will definitely have ear infection trouble due to training conditions and changes in climate; or if you want to take the risk, you can stay in the Navy."

Two small reasons caused me to choose to stay. An infamous Navy barber had already cut off my hair. My heavy curly locks lay on the barber shop floor. I was nearly bald. I could not think of returning to my home town looking such a sight. The second reason was not any more valid. Going through the high pitched business of enlisting, saying goodbyes, and going off to fight for my country, simply could not be so easily retracted. I must stay in the Navy at all costs. Later in a reflective moment, I've wondered if I caused one of my mother's prayers to go unanswered. I'm sure she was praying that at least some of her six sons would not have to go to war.

Boot camp at Farragut, Idaho was followed by hospital corp school in San Diego, and after brief hospital experience in Seattle, I was shipped out to the South Pacific. Thousands of hospital corpsmen followed a very similar pattern. Many ended up as I did in the fleet marines. Fleet marine training saved my life – not only during the war, but more than once since. Men who had fought on the front lines and survived were our instructors. Only one objective was in their minds – to give us the kind of survival training that would save our lives in actual combat. Only admiration remains for the tough, driving, combat-proven, leather necks. A special fiber was woven into our youthful character. Bob Bush, a close buddy, won the nation's highest honor for bravery, above and beyond, saving lives of the wounded on the battlefield. On Guadal Canal, cool action saved my own life, under conditions that took lives of men all around me.

Twice since the war, that training kept me alive under extremely dangerous conditions. At 12,000 feet above the Canadian Rockies, the single engine on my V-tailed Beechcraft Bonanza failed. Only perfect presence of mind brought my wife, daughter, and self out of the broken clouds alive. Calm, born of training, helped me perform the right procedures while keeping the dead-engined aircraft level and under control. The Bonanza did start again. We broke out beneath the clouds at 11,000 feet between the mountains over the Banff, B.C. highway near the Isenhour.

On another occasion, the waters of the Pelly river, swollen by spring run-off, battered the log raft I was on during an attempted crossing. Deep in the heart of British Columbia, the river remained the last barrier to a successful journey by some friends and myself. The raft could not be anchored after our crossing, and the angry racing river swept us away from the bank and into the powerful current. My days as a Navy life guard, jumping in full combat gear from ship decks and other wartime experiences, helped me survive the wild river. Some on that raft were not so fortunate.

Guadal Canal was already secured when I arrived. The marks of death were still there. The Tenearu cemetery, with its thousands of white crosses, gave silent testimony of the young marines who gave their lives in the island-hopping jungle war of the South Pacific. Those were the days of the broadcast of Toyko Rose, a midwest U.S. girl turned traitor. One of her sinuous broadcasts ended with these words. "If you don't think Japan is still in the war, ask the boys on Guadal Canal."

I was one who knew what the "Black Rose" was talking about. Two hundred sixty-one men had been blasted into eternity the night before in the Guadal Canal Harbor. A heavily loaded U.S. ammunition ship, due to sail that night, was hit by a Japanese torpedo. I was blown out of my bed by the concussion of the explosion less than a mile away, but my life was saved when two banks of steel lockers fell toward each other across my bed. Braced against each other, the lockers took the impact of the shrapnel that ripped across the harbor end of the island. I first believed Japanese war ships were shelling the island in preparation to retake this bloody turning point of the South Pacific War. Two minutes later, all was quiet. The next morning, our grizzly work began. Only one man who was aboard the ill-fated ammunition ship survived. He was blown 400 yards out to sea in a top side bosun locker. The seaman was alive in the warm tropical water, suffering from shock and surprisingly, pneumonia. My duties for several days were to take special watch over this lone survivor. He did live to appear on Ripley's "Believe it or Not" a few months later.

It was on Guadal Canal, which in normal times was a far away tropical paradise, that I faced my "Damascus Road experience." Like the great Apostle Paul, centuries before, I was arrested by God. For me, this was the most eventful aspect of the war. Half way around the world from home, I made the decision that totally shaped my life from that moment on. At that point in my existence, I helped make up the huge army of nominal Christians who had made no deep commitment to Jesus Christ or his claims. Gladly I accepted His provisions, but not His plan.

The day God confronted me concerning acceptance of His will in my life started as had many of my days on that South Seas tropical island. The island war had moved north. Except for an occasional isolated attack from Japanese hiding deep in the jungle, and the devastating sinking of the ammunition ship, we now lived in minimal danger on Guadal Canal. My duties at the advanced naval medical station were light. In order to battle boredom, free time had to be managed. The secret was to crowd as many activities into each day as a few of us close buddies could invent. M.A.S.H., and a few other assorted conglomerations of what service life was like back then, hadn't been invented yet. The key and secret to keeping zest in what could have been life in Dullsville was in inventiveness. Our challenge was to simply capitalize on the opportunities available to us, and a few that were not available. Extra food we could manage. Our medical dispensary had a degree of priority and so the chow list may have included a few patients long since discharged or even fictional in nature. Vehicles were no problem either. Friends in the motor pool were always there in case there was a jam up for the two or three vehicles assigned to our station. Racing on the abandoned airfield, no longer in use in personal carriers, was among the diversionary events we enjoyed. A simple obstacle course involved driving near the control tower while avoiding being bombed by coconuts thrown from above. Timed driving events carried risk with them – not only the danger of too much speed on the narrow roads, but also the M.P.'s who vowed to shut down the speedsters if caught. The rules were simple: visit some friends a fair distance away, wait until minutes before curfew, then race the clock to home base. We called in to give our starting times. One of the great secrets of the war was how we avoided detection and action by the M.P.s.

Trading with the local and imported South Sea natives generated another challenge. The scantly clad natives aided in malarial control by cutting the tall grass among the sluggish jungle streams. Armed with a sack of service rations and other acquired food, we would make our way to the native villages or encampments. Carvings, walking sticks, and weavings were well crafted. One of my buddies wanted a very nicely carved mother of pearl inlaid walking stick. Approaching the owner, whose dyed blond hair stood at least eight inches straight up on his head, my friend began vigorously bargaining in pigeon English. I could hardly understand him myself. Pointing, making signs and showing items for trade, my pal only confused the native, and myself for that matter. Finally, the blonde black man put up his hands, and in perfect English said, "Listen Joe, if you want to buy my cane, let me know what you have to trade. Maybe we can make a deal!" We emptied our sack of trading goods and acquired the walking stick.

On the night I met God, the day concluded with one of the most beautiful tropical sunsets I had seen in the islands. In the afternoon, a fellow only a few weeks resident on the island felt to do something about my lukewarm spiritual state. This cherubic appearing zealot belonged to a Bible verse memorizing group called Navigators. God may have sent him to Guadal Canal just to get me tracking spiritually. "Come with us to the Tenearu Chapel tonight, Clarke," my new divine mentor ordered. "There's a navy chaplain going to be speaking. He's good!" I wondered mildly, "Good by whose standards." The walk wouldn't hurt, and I wanted to see the beautifully built chapel up close. The chapel had been designed and built by South Seas islanders as part of the cemetery and as a memorial to the thousands of marines who died in one of the key actions that turned the tide of the war with Japan.

I refused a ride or any company as I headed out on the 20 minute walk to the evening service. Dusk dropped like a velvet mantle over the green paradise. Night followed instantly. I was by myself on the well-defined trail only a few hundred yards from the bamboo Chapel. I was not alone. It was as if dozens of fireflies were assigned to keep me company. How these tiny blinking fluorescent lights managed their magic, I could only imagine. There was suddenly something else with me on that dark path. A voice! I was more startled than frightened. I was given a message loud and clear. "You cannot serve two masters!" That voice pierced into my conscience. I knew I wasn't going all out to be a witness for God, but I certainly didn't feel I was doing much to serve the devil. I had been coasting as I saw it, sort of on furlough. Time enough to gear up again when the war was over. God thought otherwise. He had just taken away my "no man's land!" Shaken, I picked up my pace, reached the chapel, entered and dropped into a canvas bottomed chair, three rows from the front. Others were still arriving, my buddies and the fellow who had invited me were across the aisle a row closer to the front. Having put my pocket New Testament in my shirt before coming, I took it out and idly thumbed through its crisp new pages. The little book seemed to lock open at Luke the 16th chapter. Puzzled, I stared at the page and verse 13 seemed to rise up from the flat sheet. "No servant can serve two masters; either he will hate the one and love the other..." Unsettled, I shut the hot little book and put it back in my shirt pocket. I didn't dare look around; this was too much.

      Singing in Navy chapel services lacked everything I was used to in the Pentecostal church back home. Mumbling along on "A Mighty Fortress is Our God," I was in a total state of flux. God had thoroughly shaken my complacency. Now the Chaplain took the small pulpit to speak. He didn't appear to be the type one might expect to be a minister in what I considered a more formal church. Pentecostal preachers were different. They came rough, gruff, poorly trained and often with limited mastery of the Queen's English. What the Pentecostals lacked in polish, they made up in power of conviction and persuasion. This Navy Chaplain was like a surgeon – precise, directed, with keen purpose. I was not prepared for his approach to speaking. He drove his scalpel directly into my heart – reading from

Luke 16:13, the very words I had already twice faced this same night. I felt like Peter may have when the Lord told him, "Before the cock crows twice, you'll deny me thrice."

"Some of you fellows have been hiding out on God on this island," the Chaplain told us. "I'm here to tell you tonight that you can't get away with it. God wants your witness to be strong, not hidden." I had been had. Upon invitation by the straight shooting chaplain, I went forward and confessed. Yes, like Jonah of old, I had been hiding out on God. The deep commitment I made to Jesus Christ that night, I have kept.

The round faced, cherubic zealot became my mentor. I did not join The Navigators, but I did begin to memorize scripture, to be open and testify to my faith, and the Lord Jesus' claim to my life. Two scriptures I memorized in those following weeks on Guadal Canal have helped carry my faith all the days since. "I know in whom I have believed....and I am persuaded that He is able..."

The hell bomb dropped at Hiroshima and Nagasaki brought the Pacific War to an abrupt end. Victory over Japan day came and the war was over. The Axis defeated, tens of thousands of U.S. service men began streaming back home. Like the small boy who called his parents from summer camp to tell them he was going to get to ride home in an ambulance, I came home to San Francisco Harbor on a hospital ship. A small series of medical problems gave me priority and a berth on the air conditioned mercy ship. Lingering malaria, fungus, ear infection and acne from heat-stimulated sebaceous glands made up the entries in my thick medical file. My Navy discharge came from the Oakland Bay Naval Hospital. Armed with a small pension, and mustering outpay, I was headed north on a bus similar to the one that had carried me from home nearly four years before.

A sense of euphoria gripped me as the Greyhound bus sped northward through California's Mount Shasta area into the lush valleys of coastal Oregon. Somewhere in mid Oregon, strong, quiet thoughts seemed to beam their way into my consciousness. It was as if I was listening in on the prophecy of my own future. "You will return home and prepare yourself for college." Until that moment, I had given no thought to what I would do once back in the small apple valley of my youth. Omak, my home town, seemed smaller and Main Street much shorter, than I remembered. No one met me at the bus stop. It really didn't matter! I was home, safe and sound, really almost unscarred by the war. Mother, my step-father, Willis, and brother Neal and his family were living somewhere in the California Sacramento Valley, and I walked the few blocks to the new address and small house that would now be home. With very little ceremony, I removed my Navy blues, found some Levis, and stepped back onto the street leading to Main. I must walk, reflect, drink in the tiny realm I had missed and dreamed of month after month while I was gone. A note left by brother Russell let me know he was home but away visiting. I would see him in the morning.

The night air was pleasant, and I walked along relaxed in no hurry. Just to walk Main Street past the post office, Omak Chronicle, Nash's Pharmacy, and Bramer's Hardware, was a return to the familiar. Past Penny's and the theater, I received my first shock! The James J. Hill Hotel was gone! The historic landmark with its cedarbloom super creamed ice cream shop, vanished. I stood transfixed, staring at the new structure that replaced the grand thick walled old place. It was as if someone had burned up some of my memories. My job at Cedar Blooms, my classmate Carole, and the place the hotel had served as a high school gathering center – gone! After long moments, I turned back to walk to the strange little house under the shadow of the hill at the edge of town.

Reaching the house slightly tired, after a day of travel and the walk on Main Street, an awareness slowly made its way from somewhere deep in my mind into a conscious thought. Something was different. Most things were the same, but something was definitely different. It wasn't just the absence of family or the surprisingly small number of people I recognized on Main Street. It was more than that! Maybe tomorrow I'd go to the high school, look around, find out what happened to Rachel, my childhood sweetheart. Even as these thoughts passed through my mind a stronger clearer knowledge and understanding struck me. Things would never be the same again—not at church, nor with Rachel, or with family. The umbilical cord to my former life had been cleanly cut. I had left four years before a boy. I came back a man. My life would now be found in the future, not the past.

He who strives... who spends himself and who, at worst, fails while daring... shall never be with those cold and timid souls who know neither victory nor defeat.
–Teddy Roosevelt

1 Timothy 2:3-5 (KJV)

... Endure hardness, as a good soldier of Jesus Christ. No man that warreth entangleth himself with the affairs of this life; that he may please him who hath chosen him to be a soldier... if a man strive for masteries, yet he is not crowned, except he strive lawfully.

CHAPTER EIGHT

CLIMBING TOWARDS SUCCESS

Enrolling in Central Washington State, then known as a College of Education, was brother Russell's choice, not mine. Ironically, he transferred to Bellingham after a year, and went on to the University of Washington. I stayed at Central and found the school much to my liking. There were several reasons why I succeeded in college – not because anyone expected me to do so. A prediction or two that college was too big an undertaking for me, circulated around back home. Being middle-man academically in my high school class was not exactly a great credential. None of my older brothers had even finished high school. Russell was a much better bet as he had tied with a couple others as the top of his class.

Four years out of high school, I started college far more directed. I was settled down, maturity was setting in. Romantically, I was unattached. Girls were a great delight, but not a fatal fascination. The real secret to my success was my absolute knowledge of the necessity of total application of study. I had no illusions whatever that charm, or previous popularity would help one iota. My approach to books and college courses was utterly serious. I survived, when more endowed students were forced to drop out due to poor grades. I knew I was flat out an average student – perhaps the ultimate model of the average man. My grades did improve the longer I stayed in colege, and eventually seeing more B's than C's, and even the occasional A on my card, was most gratifying. Six years later, I had acquired a BA in physical education, an elementary and secondary teaching certificate and my Masters degree in education administration. A general teaching certificate plus a thesis in counseling helped me face the world of my productive years better prepared.

The toughest challenge in college was making it in athletics. I had only three handicaps. I was too small, too slow, too poorly prepared, and even a little late in getting a start. One hundred sixty-five big men showed up for starting football practice. Some of these men were veterans, like myself. Many of them had experience on service teams. Only one quality kept me on the grid iron beyond the first week of grueling, meat-grinding, workouts – determination! Down from my high school weight of 190 pounds, with no training table, or such a thing as pumping iron, the tackle position I played in high school was out. The line coach switched me to pulling guard, trying to help me find a nitch. The fact that I hung on to make the 33 man traveling squad was a small miracle.

A pattern was established that I could not break in all my efforts to succeed in college sports. Just as I felt I had worked hard enough to make the squad, an injury would occur to force me out. In football, a cracked collar bone ended my freshman efforts. In track, after working on the 440 run and relay team, my left big toenail, injured in childhood, turned black and came off. In basketball, the final injury which ended my efforts in college athletics, ocurred in scrimmage, while going up for a lay-in, I was pushed into the brick wall at the end of the practice gym. My right knee cracked and I went down; out of all further hopes of competition. The injury played a part in the turn my life took in my last years of college.

Three things happened during my sophomore year that would have to be considered monumental in the turn my life took at that time. Margi came back into my life, I learned to fly an airplane, and I received a divine call to Gospel ministry.

Lying in the college infirmary with a badly swollen right knee, too painful to walk on, I had time to think. Things were veering a bit off course from my plans! Thoughts of a business major were soundly torpedoed by a subject called "Business Statistics." Barely passing the course, and with the promise of more frightening subjects to come, I retreated into the area of animal husbandry. Then hours of chemistry and the threat of biology and related subjects brought me to reality. My high school counselors were right – my talents lay in the field of human relationships and not in math and science. Aptitude tests had shown my interest in people-related endeavors. Fortunately for me, all subjects I had taken so far were required or counted as electives. Moving into the education department was right. Once back on my feet, I was sure I finally knew where I was heading.

The flying began naturally. A 2-year-old, 65 horse power Taylorcraft came into my possession through a trade with my lifetime friend, Dick. Dick was now married, and the small aircraft seemed a lesser priority to Dick and his wife, Marrion. A piece of property I owned with a house on it perfectly fit their needs. Free to roam, I needed wings. I traded the property for the airplane, and cash to boot, and began taking lessons. Soloing in six hours, I began hopping back and forth between college and my home in the upper Okanogan Valley. The real use of my flying would come years later – by a "divine call" to ministry, I mean hearing an audible voice speak to me, saying, "I have a purpose for your life, and a work for you to do!"

During a weekend at home, I attended the church to hear a healing ministry named Velmer Gardener – a look alike for the better known William Branham. The era of the great healing crusades was in full swing and gaining momentum. My knee was stiff and painful as I hobbled into the crowded building and was soon caught up in the highly charged atmosphere of the meeting. Most of the healers of the era were good preachers, the lust for money and acclaim would not take some of them for yet another decade. Before their times passed, I sat in the auditoriums and tents or on the platform as sponsor to most of the prominent names. A.A. Allen, in his early days, was an effective and anointed man. William Branham remained the epitome of a spiritual giant to the end. Oral Roberts, whom I helped sponsor for a great meeting in the Yakima Valley, turned his operation into a highly polished, perfectly organized machine early on. Katherine Kuhlman, Jack Cole, Gordon Linsey, and dozens of lesser lights, burned brightly during the great wave of healing sweeping the late forties and fifties.

My knee was healed the night Velmer Gardner prayed for me. Getting into the front part of the healing line, as it was called, I was about the sixth or seventh to be prayed for. The main evidence that something had happened to my knee was the great reduction in pain I felt. I knew I had received a healing touch. We were encouraged to thank God for our healing, so many of us went into a large prayer room behind the platform for a time of thanksgiving. I had no more than knelt on my newly healed knee when the "Voice" I had heard once before on far away Guadal Canal spoke again to me. "I have a purpose for your life," I was told, "I have a work for you to do!" Soon, the understanding came as to why a career in business was not for me. Even being a gentleman farmer as a result of my studies in animal husbandry, was not to be. My calling was to be with people. A further word from God that came later was, "The good you do for Me, you will do for people."

Margie, a tall beautiful, radiant Christian, "every inch a lady," came back into my life after nearly a ten-year absence. We had enjoyed a good youthful friendship in all the innocence of the unblemished young – holding hands maybe, a kiss absolutely not! Margie had actually attended Central Washington College for two years while I was away winning the war. Obviously, others had considered the sheer delight of one of Margie's kisses. She was voted the girl with the most kissable lips in college. Other girls could have won "the most kissed" title. With Margie, they could only dream.

My transportation department in those days included, beside the T-craft, a model A Ford four-door, and a classic '39 green Buick special. Russell and I had our order in for a new 1948 Buick at the Anderson Buick Agency in Wenanchee, Washington. We were number six on the list. Our turn just never came up. We did, after waiting many months past our due date, ask Mr. Anderson if someting was required beyond the sizeable deposit we had already paid. Our question was not well received, and negotiations began to end the long delay. Our deposit bought the sleek, perfectly conditioned '39 Special. The wartime retreads came off one at a time, usually in one long piece requiring new replacements, not yet too easily obtained. The Buick was a jewel. In nostolgic moments, I regret not keeping the T-craft, Model A Ford, and sleek green Buick. The trio would now, at today's prices, greatly defray the cost of a modest college education.

My attendance at a mid-winter Okanogan Valley Youth rally was the occasion for seeing Margie again. I had driven the green Buick to my home town Omak for the weekend, learned of the Saturday night rally, and decided to attend. Space in my Buick Special filled up with six young ladies from the Omak Assembly. The least I could do was provide transportation for these needy ladies. I can't say I was totally void of interest in at least two of them. The Oroville Assembly, forty miles north, was packed with young people by the time we arrived and parked. Only a front seat remained, so I followed the six young women, single file, the full length of the aisle and into the front seat. Margie's sister, an English missionary type, was guest speaker. Margie and her mother were seated halfway back on the left side of the auditorium. Margie, of course, and three or four hundred others, observed the spectacle of my grand entrance with my bevy of young ladies. I'm sure Margie's sister, Marie, preached a great word on the need for youthful commitment. I'm sure much of it was lost on this crowd of vibrant youth, caught up with each other and the excitement of life itself. One on one teaching may still be the best way to help bring deep personal commitment to fruition in the young. I stood and turned to face the crowd after dismissal and saw Margie half way back on my right. I still believe only a Hollywood screen test would have proven whether Margie was or was not every bit as beautiful as screen star Ingrid Bergman, also of the same Swedish decent. My entourage of young ladies had made their way out by the same route as we had entered. I had only a few minutes in order not to be conspicuously late for task as chariot driver returning the ladies back home to Omak. Moving down the right aisle, I greeted Margie's mother first and then turned to look fully into the deep blue eyes of the woman Margie I had never known. Incredibly, Margie had just returned from a bank job in Seattle and was unmarried. Our visit was brief, nothing was stated or implied, but somehow everything was settled. I knew that night that I would see Margie again, and that something more would follow. Margie admitted later that a flash of unexplainable jealousy swept over her as she caught sight of me following the six girls to the front of the church that night.

A small note in my mail, back at college a week or two after the youth rally, sent me north at Easter time to see Margie. She merely mentioned that she had enjoyed seeing me at the rally, and that she would be home at Molson for the coming spring and summer. Like a hungry stream trout looking for food, I leaped at the tempting thought of seeing Margie again. A letter and a phone call from me brought a casual, "If you happen to be up this way, drop by." It was hardly a drop by! Margie's parent's cattle ranch lay at four thousand feet elevation hidden in the Okanogan high lands. One last call, for exact directions, and I left Omak for the sixty plus mile drive to Margie Molson's ranch home. Dinner was to be at 6:00 p.m., and I nearly made it on time. A late spring, six inch snow fall, once I climbed the seemingly endless grade, was no help. Missing the turnoff and taking an unplowed, little used road was my next problem. Getting stuck made matters worse. A slight bit late, and disheveled, I arrived, but I was sure that I had done the right thing once I caught sight of Margie. Margie's bachelor brother, old maid sister Marie, and mother, were discreetly at the edge of things as a sumptuous meal was served in the seldom-used dining room on best dishes and silverware.

Margie looked radiant that night. The full boom of youth and health was in her face. A woman with training and work place experience, Margie was the picture of beautiful maturity. It was obvious she was still in love with quiet country living. Margie studied me as I recounted my war experiences as well as college progress. Was there a real John Clarke behind my appearance and account of myself? That night, I decided I wanted to marry Margie. I planned, on our next meeting, to ask her if she would.

Back in classes at C.W.C.E. my life came together. Courses followed in meaningful order. My campus Christian testimony flourished. I began speaking and witnessing to the athletes whose ranks I never quite made. Elected President of the strong campus Intervarsity group, I spent part of the following summer at "campus in the woods," in the far away Lake of Bays area in Ontario. Exposure to Carl Henry, Don Troutment, Dr. McNeary of Union Theological Seminary, and other oustanding leaders, left a profound impression on me. Knowing I would have little time to work during the summer, it was clear that funds for my junior year would be short. It occurred to me that a simple, partial solution would be to save as much as I could of the nearly five hundred dollars of expense money I had been given by the college Intervarsity group. Answer? Hitch hike! And this I did, for nearly seven thousand miles in all. My great disappointment of the entire saga was that not one ride did I obtain in a Cadillac. I did ride on the back of an empty auto transport truck, swaying and whipping around corners at high speed, bent on dislodging me, yes! Another truck I was riding in North Dakota, loaded with pipe and bound for the oil fields out west, caught on fire on a down hill. The driver and myself leaped off at the edge of a small town as the truck's flaming brakes started a grass fire. The local fire department came to the driver's rescue, as I retrieved my suitcase and went back on to the highway to continue hitch hiking rides west. I prayed a special prayer at this time for good rides. Only a few days remained before Russell and his fiancee, Ruth's summer wedding. I needed to be there to serve as best man, for my brother and truest friend. My prayer was answered the same day – I hitched one ride for seventeen hundred miles, and was dropped off within fifty miles of my home town. I stepped out of the vehicle I had helped drive day and night, under the shadow of the vast Grand Coulee Dam. A few hours later, I was in Omak, ready for Nuptial practice and wedding ceremony two days later.

Money in my pocket from a providential late summer job, plus over three hundred saved by hitch hiking, allowed me to return to college in some solventcy. College wrap up suddenly began to accelerate. What was before exciting but leisurely, was now moving at an unexplainable faster pace. Before, things like studies, activities, and trips to the valley sort of happened. Now things were directed on purpose, planned. Grades were sought not to do well and pass a class, but for a reason. I had never thought of specific goals before now. I was no longer going to school because I should, or because my brother had. It was as if I had come out into the broad light of day. Life in many ways had been a fog bank of random events. The ties that were cut during the service years were never attached again. I had no home church where I was tied in. Family was scattered, with no gathering strength of close relationships. It is one thing to become a man, quite another thing to become mature with relationships and purpose.

Margie came into my life at a destined moment. On our next meeting I asked Margie if she would consider a serious relationship with me. I received a very direct question in response. "How can you be so sure so quickly?" No, I didn't say something religious ike, "God told me so!" I simply said I was sure and was willing to wait for Margie to be satisfied that it was true. I could say I had no other girl in mind. It may have been Margie's 13-year-old nephew, David, and her dog Scrappy, that turned the tables in my favor. I found myself very much in love with Margie, and set out to win her heart. It required my full resources to court this former Apple Blossom Princess from the Molson Hills. I pressed my full resources into action. Airplane, Buick, and even the Model A Ford, just for a change of pace, were used. The long seven mile grade from the valley floor to the Molson Highland was nearly the undoing of the Model A Ford. I only made that mistake once. The Taylorcraft airplane was faster, and proved more capable of meeting my needs. Margie's father, a cattle rancher with an operation using locations in three countries, complicated matters. Margie might be at Molson in the north, or on a ranch in the Grand Coulee Dam area, or to the far south of Washington State on a ranch near Toppenish. The routine went something like this – make a phone call, race to the airport, take off to the sky and head north or south to find Margie. Thirteen-year-old David became the watch tower when my flight took me up the Okanogan and into the Molson Hills. From the chicken house roof, David would spot my red with black trim Taylorcraft when it was only a speck several miles south. By the time I landed on the strip cut along the meadow edge, David would have Margie there in the family auto to pick me up. David was on my side. So was Scrappy, Margie's slightly temperamental pet dog.

For no known reason, Scrappy took a likeing to me, when he would growl and show his disapproval to many others who stepped foot on his domain. Margie concluded that if a child and a dog whom she loved approved of me, she would have to at least give me a chance. Thus my summer job was painting the large two-story family farm house. For nearly six weeks I painted on the great house – two coats everywhere, including the roof and the well house, and even the outhouse still used for emergencies, now with the advent of indoor plumbing. Time seemed to present itself for fishing and horseback riding. Margie and I would ride to some high place on the sprawling four to five thousand acre ranch, through wheat fields and pasture. We could view the distant valley below, with its silver string of a river, and even the faint outline of the mountains beyond. I began to love these high hills and the ranch home that stood in the meadows below. Margie was a part of it all. Patches of flowers and berries, groves of quaking aspens and deep stands of tall evergreens seemed placed by an artist's touch. I can still in my mind see Margie sitting easily and straight on her favorite steed, years of riding experience showing in the perfect understanding between woman and horse. The sun formed a golden crown at the crest of her long thick brunette hair. Blue eyes shone with love and life. Margie said "yes" that summer, and I became the most fortunate man I knew. At Thanksgiving time we became engaged, with a June wedding in mind. Her ring I earned that fall doing something I was good at, picking apples. Our money for the honeymoon and beginning life together came in the spring. I contracted to thin apples and was able to have several hundred dollars by the day we were married.

The full promise of summer was upon the valley on June 25th, and the promise of a fuller life upon Margie and me. We exchanged vows on my mother's birthday and honeymooned in beautiful British Columbia. Penticton, Suswap Lake, Lake Louise, and the Kootenay Lakes sealed our love forever with the wonderful splendor of the land north of the border. Margie and I began life together in a log cabin we reconstructed on her parent's ranch. Reconstructed is exactly what we did – dismantling the cabin I owned nearly one hundred miles away. A most generous brother loaded them on his logging truck and delivered them to the Molson Hill Ranch. We reassembled the numbered logs, chinked the cabin, put in windows and doors. An old man who had known Margie from childhood split shakes by hand, and placed them on the cabin roof as a wedding present. Fall came, and we found ourselves heading for Central Washington State College for my senior year.

Few experiences in life are as pleasant as being a senior. That place, truly earned, is sweet. The hard task of proving academic capability for me was won. The assurance of graduating was comforting. The task set to, and finished, carries a level of confidence never lost. With Margie by my side, I felt ready to challenge life, and seek a mountain to climb.

I searched the green valley, I walked in the woods, I ran by the seashore. I stood on a high cliff. I wondered in this heart of mine if ever I would find joy for my spirit and peace in my mind. The search was not in vain.

Numbers 14:7-8

... *The land, which we passed through to search it, is an exceeding good land. If the Lord delight in us, then He will bring us into this land, and give it to us; a land which floweth with milk and honey.*

CHAPTER NINE

THE GOOD YEARS

Margie and I stood quietly viewing a small two door Chevrolet coupe that was sitting on the local Chevrolet show room floor. We were not given much notice by the two or three salesmen moving about looking busy but keeping their eyes sharply focused on a few older prospects. My wife and I were looking for our first new auto. I had sold the green '39 Buick in order to give my brother Russell his share of the original investment. The Taylorcraft flying machine was also in the hands of another owner. Margie had worked as secretary in the registrars office during my senior year, thus we had the cash to buy our first car. Since we both wanted a Chevrolet similar to the one displayed by the Ellensburg dealer, we stayed around longer than one normally would when salesmen fail to even see you. Picking up a pamphlet, Margie and I found the exact model, and a two-tone color we liked. Maybe we could go home and call the auto company owner to see if we could order the nifty two-tone coupe. As we headed for the door an older salesman called out to us. "Hi kids, they sure look great don't they?" It was obvious none of the salesmen expected a couple our age to have enough money for a new car. We did order the two-toned coupe, and decided to take delivery at the factory. The older car salesman was on hand when Margie and I walked into the Chevy Agency a few days later to pay for our auto order. "You young people interested in a car?" he asked. "No" we said, "we are here to pay for one we have already purchased." "You, what?" He stood and stared, as we placed a bank draft for nearly two thousand dollars on the counter in front of the cashier. "I didn't know those kids had any money," he muttered to the cashier as we were leaving the showroom. "Who took their order?" I'm sure the salesmen found out that we called the owner to place our order. He may have also received some pointers in how to pick out cash customers.

Paying cash for our first automobile set a general pattern for Margie and me – whenever possible, we paid cash. New philosophies have by now replaced the old way prudent people used to conduct their business affairs. For Margie and me, paying cash for that little Chev coupe began our journey through the good years.

What a grand country! Such history and people! No land is quite like this land! The train carried Margie, baby and myself eastward out of our lush, fruit growing valleys, past the great bread basket of the world, the grain lands of the Poluse, into vast Montana and finally, through the Dakotas and on to the land of ten thousand lakes. The picturesque dairies of Wisconsin came next, then Chicago. We were not ready for Chicago. I don't think a person could ever be ready for Chicago. I think of Chicago as a sprawling giant by the lake ready and just waiting for all comers. Getting off the train in the great station with no idea as how to get into Flint, Michigan, became a challenge. On the map the distance didn't appear to be far. At first we sat in the main station with our luggage just wondering what to do. Baby Beth chose this moment to get sick. Total strangers, in a huge city, and not knowing a soul, knowing we couldn't catch a bus with a sick baby, we needed some place to stay. I called a minister of our fellowship and told him our plight. He couldn't help, but gave us a phone number to a missionary rest home. This proved to be the perfect answer for us. The home was nearby and people were willing to come take us there. Warm, friendly and caring, that Chicago missionary rest home was an angel of God to us.

Beth remained sick only long enough for us to meet the delightful people who ran the home, and the several veteran missionaries staying there at the time. We had two restful night's sleep and were taken to the bus to continue on to Flint. Beth put on a special show after her rapid recovery that helped pay for our stay in the rest home. She entertained, laughed at everything and held out her arms to everyone who came by, to the delight of all. There was another benefit of our unexpected delay. I called the Flint factory to ask how to find them and if the car was ready. A delay had occurred concerning the paint job and the coupe would not have been ready. Our arrival at the factory was timed to the hour with the Chevy's readiness.

The trip east by train to Chicago and on to Flint to pick up the little jewel of an automobile, didn't end there. Finding ourselves farther east than either Margie and I had ever been, we decided to just go on to Boston, New York, Philadelphia, and Washington, D.C. while we were at it – being young compensates for experience. At that marvellous time in my life nothing was impossible, even with a year old baby. We gave not one thought to distances or time. The money not paid to ship the vehicle from Flint, Michigan to Washington State paid for our fare east. Once in possession of our new car we had a place to eat and sleep. With a small tent and a fold out tiny stove that used canned Sterno heat, we were totally self sufficient. Very low fuel prices at the time made such travel totally possible. At twenty plus miles to the gallon, we could cross a state for a few dollars, and so we did – many in fact.

We did drive on eastward to Boston, New York, and Washington, D.C. The nation's capital with Capital Hill, the White House, and the Washington and Lincoln Memorials, held us captive for two days before we made the final decision as to the extent of our trip. More national attractions drew us. The Virginas, Monticello, home of George and Martha Washington, Shenandoah Valley and Old Kentucky Home remained on the list we created between us. Why such a trip? What part did it play in our lives later? That nearly ten thousand mile trip proved to be the shades of things to come. My ministry since has logged hundreds of thousands of miles. But that would all come later.

Margie and I sat in our tiny four wheel home, with Beth sleeping in the back seat, on the sunny well-kept grounds of the Old Kentucky Home, studying a map. Suddenly Washington state and home looked a long way away. A little of the steam that had carried us so far, seemed to have leaked out. We struck out for Missouri, Kansas and Colorado. When we came to Wyoming, enough enthusiasm still remained to detour to Yellowstone and see if Old Faithful was for real.

Back in the Yakima Valley at Margie's parent's home, the full measure of the trip we had just taken came to us. Six weeks had sped by and nearly ten thousand miles. The second night home Margie and I had a most unusual simultaneous nightmare. Lights from nearby Toppenish, Washington were shining into the upstairs bedroom window where we were sleeping. In my dream the light reflection on the floor appeared slick and watery. I was sitting up in bed with my left hand on the bed post at the foot of the bed. My right hand had the rail in a vice like grip. This to me was the steering wheel. Margie also was sitting up alongside of me and had her left arm locked through my right arm telling me to be careful. "I am," I told her sharply! Margie woke up first and started laughing. Still caught in this most dangerous driving situation, I could see nothing funny and told Margie so. I woke up a few seconds later and the whole thing had us laughing in hysterics for a good part of the night.

Two years had passed since graduation, including a year teaching and coaching in the tiny hilltop home village near Margie's home on the ranch. Our second year out of college, we were forced to make a monumental decision. The Central Washington College president's office called to tell me I had been selected for a scholarship. Work done could count toward a master's degree and placement opportunities would be excellent, after completion of the program. As has happened several times since, a choice had to be made between ministry to the people of God or furthering the teaching career to which I could have easily devoted a lifetime. The ironic thing about the master's program offer is that it came on the heels of a very insignificant opportunity to travel in the state of Colorado with Margie's minister sister, Marie. The Colorado trip would have Margie and me helping in services in a number of very small churches. I would play my trumpet, sing specials with Margie, and lead song services. Marie and another woman preacher would deliver the sermons. When the spokesman for the college president asked if I would accept the scholarship, I said I would be driving though the town where the school was located a few days later and would give the President my answer in person. The dilemma I faced was how could I refuse the training program, and give a credible reason for doing so? Picturing something equivalent to the oval office in Washington, D.C., I could imagine how the questioning by the college president would go. "Well, John Clarke, have you made up your mind to accept the scholarship?" "Dr McConnel, I'm sorry but I can't do so." Next question: "Why not? What will prevent you from doing so?" Now, the impossible part of the imaginary discussion. Somehow, an answer like, "I'm going to go to Colorado and be a song leader for two lady preachers" didn't seem adequate. No good answer came to mind. To deepen my quandry, I had a short dream during this period of time. In the dream I seemed to be talking to some angelic being about this very matter. The heavenly messenger gave me a short potent thought to consider. You must go work for God now, or you never will! Nothing came to me on the several hour drive from our cabin on the ranch to the clean, small city of Ellensburg in Central Washington. Only the impossible phrase kept coming back to me, "song leader for two women preachers." However, just as we passed the city limits sign entering Ellensburg, I heard a distinct voice speak into my awareness. "You are not going to work as song leader for two lady evangelists. You are going to work for me!" Strange as it seems, that thought brought peace. I was going to go to work for God!

Mr. McConnel's office, I'm sure was not as plush as the oval office of the U.S. President, but I was impressed. The question came as I had expected. It was my answers that surprised me. I spoke in a relaxed confident way. "Dr. McConnell, I'm most honoured to be offered the scholarship. This is the highest honour I think I've ever received. The great opportunity is obvious. The reason I can't accept it is because God has called me to work for Him." The handsome white-haired president looked squarely at me for a brief instant, his blue eyes searching my face before speaking. "John, if God had called me to work for Him when I was your age, I would not be behind this desk today. Of course, you must do what He has asked you to do. What are your plans?" Nothing was said about the two lady preachers. I have some opening to minister in Colorado, I casually stated. My wife and I will be leaving soon to get started. What a start! True old-fashioned, gospel barnstorming – Margie, baby Beth, and me in our old faithful green Chevy two tone. Marie and her partner teamed up in a Pontiac four door. Places with names like Mesa, Rifle, Detas, Hotchkiss, and Graig were some of the tiny western slope towns we made one to two week stops at.

Marie and friend Gladys were women of prayer. Needless to say, Margie and I learned to pray as well. Our very livelihood depended on it. Days were spent in prayer, reading the Bible, and knocking on doors passing out our leaflets of invitations to the meetings. Small beginnings have great merit. Every new family individual who came to the meetings brought songs of great triumph. Everyone who responded to the altar call became a pure measure of joy. Twenty dollars extra over the last offering gave all of us additional times of thanksgiving. As weeks rolled into months, the itinerary came to an end and with the coming of spring, Margie and I migrated westward to home base in Washington State.

Our travels continued in our home territory. A minister friend was instrumental in arranging some meetings for us. More than a dozen engagements, sometimes at homes in Toppenish or Molson in between, filled nearly a full year. I developed a topical approach to preaching, with themes and special subjects as the heart of messages. Newspaper ads required titles so I came up with some. "The World's Last Saturday Night," "When Time Stops," and one I borrowed entitled, "I'm Going to Name the Meanest Man in Town!" I realized, if the fellow ever showed up, I could have been in trouble! I could never approach the classics I've seen put in by other evangelists. One I always envied was entitled, "Why Beautiful Women Marry Ugly Men." This sermon was on the courage of a preacher who was going to name the Anti-Christ. This was especially corageous since several Anti-Christs already named had died, leaving the title vacant.

I recieved my license to preach by mail, without attending a district council. A minister in the valley sent my name in with a recommendation that I receive a license, thus my official ministry began. Two years later at a district convention, I was ordained. Next came our first pastorate. It was as if a great door of opportunity was opened and all Margie and I had to do was to walk through it.

For some, the small church with its fifteen in attendance who unanimously elected us as the pastors, would not seem to be much of an opportunity. For Margie and me it was equal to a cathedral with a thousand member choir. We quivered with excitement seeing the great possibilities. Even the first board meeting with the two women and one man didn't discourage us. "What is your vision for the Assembly?" I asked my three board members. The two women just looked at me and said nothing. Perhaps the pain of a recent split in the church was still too great, and their faith was a bit low. The man finally spoke. "Brother Clarke," he began, "I think you and your wife are real brave to want to be our pastors. I'll tell you what I think we ought to do. We should just put a padlock on the church doors and put her out of her misery!" Unthinkable! God had called me to this town, had given me the church. No way would we give up without a battle such as that small village had never seen before. I looked back at the three board members with calm assurance, and said, "God sent me here, I believe this church can grow." Actually, that was the only thing it could do without closing the doors. From where the attendance stood, to see the bottom, we would have to look up.

Something of faith did rise up within me. "Why, I believe this church can have," I began, trying to think of a number big enough to impress my dubious board members, "over a hundred people, if we all believe and work real hard." The number I came up with even surprised me a little. But now, I was committed! Somehow, some way, one hundred people must be found and gotten into the church whatever it took! The three board members looked at me like I had promised to produce a million dollars from the sale of a half dozen pair of shoe strings.

The attendance on our first Sunday did show an increase of three over the previous week. However, this was easily accounted for by Margie, Beth, and myself. I asked for a list of absentees, drop outs, disgruntles and anyone who had visited the Assembly in recent months. I called the previous pastor who still worked in the valley as a carpenter, and asked for any ideas he might have for helping the church to grow. "Nope," he told me, "I've got no ideas. The only thing I helped the place do was to get smaller." One thing he did tell me was, we sure didn't need any of the people back who had left while he was pastor. "You don't need them," he stated strongly,. "Good riddance as far as I'm concerned." The problem the former pastor failed to take into account was obvious to me. We certainly needed some warm bodies to fill all the empty seats.

So, we set out to fill the empty pews. A necessary corresponding task, was to supplement the meager income the tiny congregation gave us. Our house was supplied, so basic food and life sustaining necessities were the two items on our priority list. Skip the luxuries and surpluses! I called Ned Phillips, the superintendent of the Natches School District to see if any teaching might be needed, part time or otherwise. To my surprise, Mr. Phillips invited me to come to his home and talk about my request. On the following Saturday morning, I drove the two miles out a paved country road through the orchard to the Phillip home. I found Ned Phillips most cordial, warm and approachable. "What can you teach?" he asked, after learning things about my background, marital state, and interests. "I think we can use you. Let me check things out. I'll need to talk to Don." Don turned out to be the high school principal. That was the end of our conversation. Not because there were not things to talk about. A sudden storm worked itself into a fury and chose a small ravine behind the Phillip's ten acre fruit orchard to produce a cloud burst. We could hear the rush of water and could only guess where it was coming from and how much. I raced out the front door and drove my car through twelve inches of swirling water to some high ground and raced back into the Phillip's house to see how I could help. Water was filling the window wells, pouring into the basement and for a frantic forty five minutes, Mr. Phillips and I lifted everything off the basement floor to a safe level above the water. As suddenly as it came, the water stopped. The damage was minimal and we found ourselves laughing at each other and the drenched state we were in. Yes I got the job teaching. Mine was a grab bag assortment of subjects including replacing the art teacher who had decided to resign at the last moment.

With housing furnished by the church and a teaching salary, Margie and I could give ourselves to building the congregation and Sunday school. There is no way to measure youthful energy, zeal and audacity. I had a good portion of each! I found a willing young evangelist of like mind, and we decided to stir things up a bit in Natches. Very few people knew anything about the church, and everybody else was happy in their oblivion. This we intended to change. People could stay away from the church, refuse to come to the church, but they could not have the privilege to be oblivious about church. My unnamed evangelist and wife began holding services in the Assembly each night. Newspaper adds began to appear in the local and valley newspapers. I bought a huge amplifier and two great speakers and announced the meetings everywhere in the small town. Next, I printed up hundreds of leaflets, rented an airplane and made like the Red Baron, bombing the village with showers of leaflets. Something would have to happen! No self respecting sedate little town would put up with such antics. Surely the one man police force would haul me in for noise pollution and littering. This didn't happen; instead, the lone policeman with his family showed up in our services and became regular attendants. We joined the Christian Life Sunday School contest and were put in the largest division category, made up of hundreds of churches of attendances between fifteen and fifty.

Students in the high school took interest and started helping out. I had them come on a Saturday morning on horseback and gave them dozens of paper plate invitations to throw on front door steps. Paul Revere never had more excitement in his race through the frontier.

The attendance did grow. First the number doubled, then tripled. It was now time to build to a climax. Mother's Day and the prettiest baby contest was nearly my undoing. What mother is going to accept the fact that her child isn't the cutest baby in town, hands down. I worked the high school dark room into a froth producing giant enlargements of each child entered and I gave so many prizes and honors no one ever really knew who won! After a month with good success it was time to produce a sure fire finale. Drop outs did reappear, disgruntled came back in spite, and new people came to check out what all the commotion was about. The final idea I'm sure came from my overworked frantic brain. The contest deadline was less than two weeks away. We wanted to top the one hundred mark, only five people from our grasp. Every night we had special music. Colored chalk drawings were given to the one bringing the most guests. I had heard that Roy Rogers had visited a California church and put that Sunday school attendance into bribe. Fortunately they were not in our category. I then knew just what we must do. We would have the

"Lone Ranger" come, impersonated! A frenzy of confusing advertisements began. I believe that a senate committee could not have castegorically proven false advertising. The day came, the final Sunday and six weeks of all our effort. The little sleepy hamlet did know about us. Even the Presbyterian pastor dropped in on a Sunday night to put his feet, as he expressed it, up to the Pentecostal fire. Pastor Tudor lived in a realm far above the aboriginal tactics of those in the class I lived in. We became good friends however, and gradually our two worlds came a little closer together.

The horse I found for our impostor, the impersonating evangelist to ride was not of "Hi Ho Silver" quality. The Lone Ranger outfit was maybe a little better. As with all good plans, small flaws do occur. How do you hold a crowd of people when the great climatic moment comes, and no Lone Ranger appears, impersonated. It seems the horse was not totally cooperative. He did lead OK and the late Ranger led him to the railing and vaulted up the steps and pushed open the front doors of the church. A hundred fifty-seven cheering record breakers welcomed him in! The impersonator strode up and down the main aisle propounding noble character building idioms like "Always ride tall in the saddle" and "Shoot straight with everyone," and "Ride alone when the crowd would take you down the wrong trail." After a few more choice admonitions, the Lone Ranger ran out the back door with the traditional "Hi Ho Silver!" well gray mare away. Startled, church arrivers stood back staring at the masked man as he leaped over the porch rail on to the old gray mare and the horse wouldn't move! A young man assigned to assist in such a case rapped the old horse on the rump with a Sunday school quarterly and off they galloped, rider hanging on for dear life. It was only a block to a pear orchard, and the horse, not heeding the pull on the reigns, took the impersonating Lone Ranger into the trees.

Another nerve racking wait occurred before the evangelist came up the back stairs and onto the platform with two or three noticeable welts on his face. The one hundred fifty-seven in Sunday school that day won the small assembly seventeenth place in the Christian Life contest. We were all ecstatic. Even the male board member beamed from ear to ear and promised to throw away the padlock he had threatened to use. The two lady board members now believed Margie and I were gifts from heaven. Three years later, the church often had a capacity attendance of over two hundred. On occasion, sixty young people from the high school would show up in Sunday morning worship services. This was to give their high school art teacher or Washington history teacher, or general business teacher, tumbling teacher, drama teacher, as the case may be, a boost.

  Needless to say, some in the good, staid, little community worried at times about this Pentecostal, high school art teacher and preacher. It was one thing for the church to grow, even to win the Community Day float parade with a "Pray for Peace in Our Valley." But where would all this lead? Slowly fears went away. The good influences seen in many young people's lives brought endorsement to my proper concern for students, beyond the walls of my classes or church. The first notable honour given me by the town of Natches was asking me to serve on the city council. I wasn't swept into politics by this duty, but must admit I did enjoy the involvement. I don't quite remember how I became the Director of Civil Defense for the area. I do remember the most extraordinary consideration we pondered regarding taking care of thousands of people who might evacuate Seattle should a nuclear shoot out begin. I don't think we ever felt sure we would be up to such a problem,

  Marilyn Gayle, our number two daughter, was born on Armistice Day, to help create a grand Thanksgiving season that year. The high school teaching job was going very well. The Natches Assembly had won the greatest growth award for any church in the northwest district. Margie and I were extremely happy together. These were indeed good years. A small question did begin to slowly form that I pondered secretly. Were these happy times enough? Was there more? Maybe even a dream come true was waiting.

What heights at what risks, or what is worth living and dying for? These measure the commitment and expendability of every challenge to life's great purpose.

Psalms 61:2 (KJV)

... *Lead me to the rock that is higher than I.*

Philemon 3:4 (KJV)

I press toward the mark for the prize of the high calling of God in Christ Jesus.

CHAPTER TEN

SPRINGBOARD TO A DREAM

The dreams of a common man or woman are equally as captivating as those of the gifted or more endowed socially or culturally. When one's world and universe is totally filled and preoccupied with thirst or hunger for accomplishment or recognition, that person is captive to a dream.

My search was not a highly directed search for great attainment. Mine was more like the moth, drawn irresistibly to the light, in a random but energetic flight. As certain elements came into play, the more likely a continued forward motion would be assured. Training led to opportunity and opportunity led to experience. Success brought notoriety and with this exposure, came greater opportunity. Additional training continued the cycle bringing more experience and always a gratifying measure of success. The pattern that followed insured a predictable eventual result.

One word described the next pastorate Margie and I accepted. Opportunity! Euphrata, located in Washington state's great Columbia Basin Irrigation Project created by the massive Grand Coulee Dam on the Columbia River, was young and raw. Thousands of migrant families looking for a place to start all over again bought the same opportunity packet – land and water and government aid to start eighty to one hundred sixty-acre farms. A number of such families made up the Assembly we began to pastor. The second word that described much of the life in the Columbia Basin was, "unfinished." Nearly everything was unfinished. The church, a new shoe box shaped building of dull, prison gray stucco, was unfinished. Stark cement steps led to an exposed outside front door. Outside steps and stairwell to the basement door were nonexistent. The basement had only two-by-four stud partitions in place. Monumental was the challenge. First, I built a porch over the front door. Next I painted the endless gray stucco exterior a soft California pink. The stairwell came next, and while resting, I attacked the forest of five foot tall thistles covering the huge lot the church sat on. The basement was last. Then we were ready to consider enlarging the congregation. Just making the changes mentioned, lifted the spirits of the stalemated congregation. Things began to rise. I bought radio time, all we could afford, and started the "shortest sermon on radio." Five minutes from beginning to end. That broadcast three times a week may have been some of the best preaching I have ever done. I'm sure I sounded just like Billy Graham with my rapid fire delivery, invitation, church address, and ten seconds of a stirring gospel hymn.

Our first promotion was to reunite a lonely airman stationed on the giant Moses Lake Air Base with his stranded wife in far away England. This sure-fire project got off to a hot start, with mounting interest and money coming in. All this we planned to bring to a stunning climax on Easter Sunday. Several things must come together besides the separated couple. Contact the wife and work out her transportation and paper work, and keep the young airman coming to church and in hand for the great moment without telling him. Of course publicity and newspaper coverage would be a prime benefit in addition to our compassionate deed of mercy. The money came in, the little wife was all set and ready to fly. Like some well-laid plans of men and mice, one tiny thing happened to smash the whole, otherwise flawless scheme. Our lonely air force husband flew the coop with another woman! Oh well, refunding the money, and making discreet explanations to well meaning participants won us respect and new members who appreciated how we handled the affair.

I nearly succeeded in the trade of a lifetime during this pastorate. Only a tricky district official thwarted my plan. Our building became too small for the growing congregation. We had to build or buy something larger. The local Seventh Day Adventist Church had just finished a beautiful Roman brick building at which time, seventy members moved away to help build another project somewhere else in the great basin area. The remaining congregation could have met on the platform of the new church. In meetings with Seventh Day Adventist pastor, we agreed to a trade, $20,000 and our building – really the deal you dream about. I contacted my district official in charge of such things and he said, "Great, if you can borrow the money." By now I was sailing. I could have won the American cup easily. I contacted a wealthy wheat farmer known for his benevolence and sure enough, I got a twenty-five thousand dollar loan. The minor details were now up to the said district official to whom I passed the loaned money. The tricky part came when the official placed the twenty-five thousand dollar loan into the account of another church project two hundred miles away. "A committee decision," he told me. Margie saved the fellow's life with counsel like, "The Bible is against man-slaughter." I did shake my head and mutter something not worth printing. In a consolation effort, I won a bid on a brick public school building no longer used, and gave the pastor who followed me a two-year project to dismantle the building, salvage the lumber, and clean seven thousand bricks. A nice addition was eventually constructed onto the existing building.

Before Margie, Beth, Marilyn, and I left Euphrata, I became involved in three further endeavors. I became a Chaplain and Captain in the Civil Air Patrol. This gave me opportunity to work with some great young people. Young people became a focus of my life as I took the directorship of a district youth camp in the Sun Lakes area of the Columbia Basin. Teaching in some capacity in the public schools, became long-time practice thereafter.

Yakima, Washington lays claim to apple capital of the world. The only ones who might question this assumption would be the Okanogan, Chelan, Wenachee and Cashmere Valleys. I think they should all enjoy the title together. In a lifetime there is often the one situation where everything comes together. For me, it seemed to have been in Yakima. The church building was new, beautiful and finished!

Marliss, our third daughter, was born and I was now surrounded with delightful females. Growing up with five brothers left me with a lifetime respect and appreciation for precious womanhood.

Forty-five thousand is a nice sized small city; just right to pull the stops and go for it. It was as if I had my hand all the way to my elbow in the proverbial cookie jar. Not just opportunity but real possibilities! I have concluded that I only want to pastor one opportunity church, for every five possibility churches. In a possibility church, everything is just waiting to happen. The opportunity church may or may not ever come together. The Yakima church came together!

First, a merger developed. Judson Cornwall, a man greatly used of God in Charismatic circles, and I tried to merge two fine congregations. The thing just didn't take. Both groups thought it was a great idea, but they just didn't want to move to the other location. Judson and I would have had a great time working together. However, no sooner did we count the negative ballots from the first attempt, than I was approached by another pastor who had a fine thriving congregation, but housed in a rickety old converted warehouse. This merger took, and I found myself pastoring more than two hundred excited people ready to go! The other pastor didn't wish to stay in Yakima, so we gathered enough funds for him and his family to relocate. My master's degree program fit in around the edges of all that was going on, completing the chapter left unfinished when I refused the college scholarship offer of a few years earlier.

"Life line," a daily broadcast every morning at nine, came about when I became involved with two businessmen in buying a defunct radio station. KBBO in Yakima can be heard today with a full menu of great listening for the Christian family. The early days of the station were touch and go, mainly because of the needs for funds. God blessed, and I started a several-year daily radio outreach. Continuing youth camp work led to becoming director of twelve district youth camps, ministering to over two thousand young people each summer. I ended up every year teaching and preaching in one or more camps as well as fulfilling director's duties.

Spiritually I was in a secure place – Spirit-filled, full gospel background, Bible preaching, doctrinally safe, soul winning, end of the world preacher. True, we were a few years ahead of times. The Charismatic earthquake wouldn't hit for

Photo Section

*My Father & Mother (center).
1918*

*My Mother Helen
at home in
South Dakota
early 1920's*

Close boy hood pal Dick Downey (left)

1935? At the Pent. Church where mom (center rear) got saved.

Camp Penelton 1944
Bottom left with Bob Bush (lower right)
winner of a Congressional Medal of Honor.

1936
With my family amid the Poverty
of the Great Depression

1939
My Buick Special with Russell
(my very close friend)

John on Rt.

*1930
My first
car
Chev
Coop*

*1940
Buick
roadmaster
with my
brother
Russell*

1943
U.S. Navy
Medical Corp.

1950
Central
Wash
State U.

Wedding to Nathel in 1973

*After the Wedding time for decision.
Which way?*

*My first Bonanza a 1950 A Model;
with daughter Marlys & Ann*

With Margie in 1960
Yakima, WA

Radio Minister during the "Good Years" at Central Assembly of God

Pastor Clarke with wife Margie
and family, Yakina, Wa, 1960.
The "Good Years."

1968. My Dream for a building on land already purchased on the freeway, Couer d'Álene, Idaho

W/wife & daughter. I Model Bonanza in which I traveled at North and South America in Ministry.

The Clarke's log cabin home near Fort St. John, in Northern British Columbia.

John and Nathel in their new life together married 1973 Couer d'Alene, Idaho.

*25
years
later*

five more years. The days of holy roller taunts and the sounds of rocks hitting the back of the Pentecostal Church would soon pass, like the Azuza Street revival, into the church archives of history. C.M. Ward, revival time, and the fastest growing full gospel church in the world, had become a tide to be reckoned with. A certain immunity seemed to protect me from a compelling desire for money. Things and gadgets I was drawn to, but in an almost rationed sort of way. Sporting items were obtained and paid for one purchase at a time. A trade for a new auto took place every two or three years. Some of my suits were now tailor-made. My wardrobe became important to me. I remained with bow ties as long as possible, but finally had to switch, under the pressure of conformance, to style.

I began to look forward to district conventions. These were times of extending acquaintanceships. I became aware of a slowly emerging corp of ministers who were on their way up. To know that I had a solid friendship with a good number of these obviously successful men was quietly gratifying. That I was sought out, and included without the agony of wanting to be, gave me private assurance. It gradually became apparent that I would be on one of the several convention committees, and even a likely candidate for one of the several district offices short of District Superintendent, Treasurer, or Secretary.

At times, I did reflect on where all of this would lead me. What would be the ultimate fulfillment for me? Could I outline my dreams of success? Under the warp and woof of my makeup, a dream was forming, but as yet I could not see its clear outline.

In all of the pleasant flow of life, family, and church work, a tiny tug would occasionally make itself felt somewhere within me. I could not tell if this thing of conscience was connected in anyway with my wife Margie's view of what ultimate spiritual growth might look like. A woman of the Spirit and prayer, Margie had concepts of life in God not held by most in the church. Deeper life we all subscribed to, even a high standard of morality and faithfulness to church programs and growth. The tug I felt may have been more than the above. Certainly there was no one I knew who could have helped me even if I had a desire to search into what even this might have been. I didn't really want to face the issue of forming a question about what might be stirring within me. I positively was as Full Gospel and Pentecostal as anyone needed to be. Another thing was clear to me. The church and I were certainly not slack in our outreach effort. We had outreaches in every direction, around the clock and month. Dozens of missionary stations blinked on our great world map in the church foyer, indicating our monetary support in many countries. The District "speed the light" program had our strong support in all kinds of youth endeavors. Locally, we had teams out each week canvassing, witnessing and ministering. The front street mission, jail, street and labor camps were places we held services. Rest homes and hospitals found us appearing regularly. Sunday school visitation found high priority on our list of urgent essentials. Our declared goal was to visit every home in the greater Yakima area. We simply had given ourselves to reaching our community for the gospel's sake. I personally preached or gave Bible studies up to ten times per week. If something was still lacking in commitment, I had no idea what it might be.

Calls began to come in for me to appear as guest speaker at different functions, a thing I truly enjoyed. Every engagement was new and different. Often I was called when others who were asked first refused or felt the assignment not to their liking.

One such invitation took me to far away Edmonton, Alberta, Canada. The occasion was a large area-wide youth gathering. I won a place forever in everyone's memory, when an illustration I used back-fired on me. My theme for the evening was the great challenge of "one" against the crowd or even the world. John the Baptist had been portrayed as the "voice of one" crying in the wilderness. The need to be able to stand alone regardless of circumstances was my theme. The illustration I chose to drive home my main point was the midnight ride of Paul Revere, the colonial American hero. I built up the account emphasizing the desperateness of the situation. It was a time of great danger and crisis! Riding at breakneck speed through the small frontier towns, Paul Revere, "the voice of only one man," cried the "British" are coming! No sooner had the word "British" come out of my mouth, when I realized that Canadians and the English had a long close mutual history. This story was similar to trying to sell Japanese war bonds in the U.S. during World War II. The laughter began slowly at first then burst into a great uproar as hundreds joined in. A sure way to gain instant affinity with a crowd is to place yourself in a position from which there is no recovery. I joined everyone in laughing, since crying was not an option. My appeal to the young people lacked the sobriety I had hoped for that night. The whole affair turned out great, and I returned, a bit wiser and more sensitive to another country and culture.

    Another unusual speaking engagement came when a local high school club sought a speaker for a gathering they had planned. A neighboring pastor was first asked and refused when the affair didn't sound very religious. The club called themselves D.E.C.A. and of course, no one had any idea what the letters stood for. Since one of the club members attended my church, I ended up with the invitation to do the speaking. A second problem causing the first pastor to decline was the fact that the gathering was to be held on a Sunday evening at the same time as the church's services. Our Lord's Day night service was also held at the same hour. I went over to the high school and attended a meeting with fifteen members of the local club. I was informed that D.E.C.A. meant Distributive Education Christian Association, simply a group of students interested in ethical business training. I agreed to speak, and began preparing for the gathering to be held in a large hotel banquet room a few days later. A guest speaker was called to cover my service that night and I made my way to the hotel not having any idea what to expect. My first surprise came in seeing a huge crowd of young people and adults gathered for the occasion. No one had told me this was a state wide gathering. I spoke that night to nearly a thousand people about bringing God into the world of business. I happened to know that the first pastor invited, had less than seventy-five souls in his service that night. I felt I had given a good set of guidelines to be passed on to all who attended that statewide D.E.C.A. meeting. I did thank God for His help that night. I ended up as the key note speaker.

Seven fulfilling years rolled by in happy succession in the Yakima Central Assembly, each 365 days filled with everything life rewards those committed to God and His people. I had given full diligence to the church and my role as pastor. It did surprise me in our seventh year with the Assembly that a stirring within me began to speak of a change for Margie and me. Our family, now complete with the arrival of a son, John Mark, loved our life in Yakima on the quiet street off Summit View Avenue. The stately brick colonial with its great back yard was a gathering place for the children's neighborhood friends and, of course, church families. How my dream made its way to the surface of my mind, is still a bit of a mystery. Perhaps it came an element at a time.

First, it seemed to me life moved in cycles and one must know on which end he is moving. I concluded that I was completing a full go in the Yakima arena, and was now ready for a much larger theater. It appeared that a man's life and career had a rhythm that must not be broken. Only a reasonable time table and window of opportunity offered itself, and one must not risk missing it. I began to outline to myself what the ultimate ideal challenge should look like. Margie was only generally informed of much of my considerations. She could be dangerous to some of my ambitions, either by praying in such a way that the thing aborted, or by quiet persuasion of sanity. One marvelous venture came down to the ground when my church secretary asked Margie if she knew I was seriously considering a very major change.

In my view, what I was considering, was not a major change, but a spectacular stepping stone. Through mutual contacts, I had been in discussions with Charles Blair, the dapper and highly inventive pastor of Denver, Colorado's sizable Calvary Temple. Much could be learned I reasoned, by working in some capacity with a ministry whose style I admired. Charles Blair and I met first in a church growth conference in Yakima. Reverend Blair, with absolutely no small talk to warm the crowd of church leaders, went directly to the heart of his subject. His opening statement began with, "Regardless of the size church you may be pastor in, just remember as I talk to you, I've pastored a church of exactly the same size at some time in my ministry." This impressed me. There was a man who could relate to every aspiring pastor. Our next meeting held in Portland, Oregon, finalized the proposition. I would resign Central Assembly, move to Denver, and become minister of Education. Three hundred fifty Sunday school teachers would be my charge, to inspire and bring forth in each commitment in depth. Charles made one thing implicitly clear. He would do the preaching. All of it!

Margie's clear logic cut the proposal into several neat pieces. Would I, John Clarke, enjoy the kind of administration assignment this would entail? Would I not miss preaching? Was God in this idea? Enough! Yes, I would miss preaching. No, I didn't like mountains of administration detail. And, how did God get into this? Wasn't all church activity God? I had already flown to Denver and gone through the mammoth Sunday school plant with it's dozens of rooms and auditoriums. My secretary read Margie my answer to Charles Blair over the phone. At lunch that day, Margie and I had a serious talk. I agreed to pray before sending the letter. The letter was never mailed, and I've never regretted not going to Denver to ride herd over the 350 Sunday school teachers.

The successful achievement of any person's dream must bring two essentials together – individual capacity matched with common sense opportunity. A few months after declining the Denver deal, I was offered a teaching position at Northwest College in Kirkland, Washington, across Lake Washington from Seattle. In chats with D.V. Hurst, the warm and enthusiastic Northwest College President, I saw the opening as just right for me. Preparing young people for Gospel ministry was a marvelous mission. I could attend the University of Washington part time and obtain an Education Doctorate. Some day, perhaps I would serve the Bible College as Dean of Education. My first teaching assignment blended freshman psychology classes with coaching the basketball team, and teaching some physical education courses. Other classes and duties would open up as the need arose.

I left Margie to sell our brick colonial house on Yakima's quiet Browne Avenue, and drove over the heavily forested mountain passes to Kirkland to prepare for classes. Planning to drive to Yakima each weekend to be with my family, I set up a sleeping cot in my gymnasium office and began to look for a house to rent during my free time.

Two weeks after college classes started, Margie called to say our Yakima home had sold. A very extraordinary thing happened at the same time. A north Seattle Church called me at the college, asking if I would consider becoming their pastor. The whole thing was unusual to this degree – each task, teaching at the college or pastoring the sizable Westminster Assembly, were full time jobs. My District Superintendent assured me I could handle both assignments. The positive college president said, "We'll work your schedule so the two responsibilities will fit together." The night after the whole matter was defined into clear terms, I laid awake on my cot in the gymnasium office pondering what the turn of events in recent weeks might mean in our family's future. Was not this the very opportunity I had dreamed of?

The Seattle area was large and beautiful. Hundreds of thousands of people lived in and around the Queen City, set on a series of hills. Westminster Church was housed in a large new building. Plans called for construction of a retirement complex to match the Sunday school, and social activity buildings. Money seemed to be no problem. Blending the two passions of my life, teaching and preaching, in a situation with vast potential, had to be the ultimate. If Margie felt the whole arrangement was right, and if the church voted yes, this would become the answer to the dream that had been many years in the making. This would become my life's greatest opportunity.

The next Sunday found my family in church at the Westminster Assembly at Seattle's 145th Avenue, Northwest. A full auditorium greeted me for my first sermon. Margie was willing and the church gave us a strong vote of approval. I stood that week on the golden pedestal of opportunity. I simply had arrived. The years of preparation had brought me to this moment. The church board agreed to begin a radio broadcast on one of the city's fifty thousand watt stations. The entire west coast could be reached over the air waves.

The pageantry of the college opening carried me, robed in black gown and red master's scarf, along into the world of academics. The church quickly pulled me into the stream of relentless growing duties and activities. I was now in the embrace of all I had ever dreamed. Only total expenditure and fulfillment could follow!

It is easier to cut free through an eight-foot wall of hardened steel with a fingernail file than to escape from a natural, temporal, world-view mindset without God!

Psalms 124:7

Our soul is escaped like a bird out of the snare of the fowlers: The snare is broken and we are escaped.

CHAPTER ELEVEN

ESCAPE

My escape into reality was not a graceful thing to behold, nor was it planned. Escape for me was divinely ordained. Houdini could not have created a more tightly fabricated escape-proof encasement than the one I had devised for myself. The whole purpose of my life for many years, in an ordered and calculated way, delivered me into my entrapment. I had successfully negotiated years of mixed metaphors in order to arrive. It was as if I had overshot the small landing field that matched my average gifts, slipped through a wind sheer, and landed beyond my destined realm. Some situations allow no miss match.

Just as a .22 shell won't fire from a .33 caliber rifle, I just wasn't matched with the highly sophisticated congregation I ended up pastoring. I have no idea if anyone other than the "Solomon wise" church secretary knew. Within weeks, my secretary, Frances, had scrutinized me through the chinks of my ill fitting armor. There was unspoken agreement between us that nothing would ever be said. I would simply self destruct in this dream impossible dilemma. All dreams have a generous portion of unreality in them; mine had more than most. The largest measure of fantasy in my dream was two fold. I would know what success would look like when it arrived, and this would give me the greatest measure of fulfillment. The intersection at which I had arrived had only superficial marks of recognition. It is so easy to read wrong when things appear so right! Everything seemed to match the blue prints of my dream. Yet, things were not quite right.

The person I had become didn't match the deepest cry of my uncomplicated heart. I was like a simple farm boy who found himself on Broadway under the bright lights, dancing to the tune not in his soul. Music to me was more like that of the true American Native. The whispered song in the tops of the swaying pine and fir trees. I connected more perfectly in spirit with the quiet forest, and the shadowy animals that lived in its hidden realms. A true cathedral for me was the needled isles between giant monarchs in the timbered sanctuaries I had frequented in my lifetime. The roaring traffic, its blurring movement and tumbling motion, was not in tune with me. The highly artificial way of life, the imposed rules of conduct required and expected, somehow fell short of true meaning. Have no fear, I would play out myself appointed to the death. I would succeed even if it killed me.

Daily I circled the northern end of Lake Washington. Mornings found me on the beautiful campus of Northwest College, teaching psychology and physical education. In the afternoon I crossed the floating bridge to begin hospital calls at the several scattered medical facilities used by the North Seattle Congregation. Nights were filled with meetings in the Church. Bible studies and prayer commanded only a token portion of the week's schedule. Board meetings, along with elders, finance, deacons, and social committees demanded prime time. Shortly after our first Thanksgiving season in the church, I was summoned to a vital, high priority social committee meeting. "This session," the chairman began, "is to begin planning on the most important event of the year." "Hum," I thought, "the nativity season must mean a lot to these people." "We need at least four major subcommittees," our chairman told us. "Dinner, decorations, entertainment, and finance members would be needed," we were informed. Volunteers popped up from all over the fairly sizeable gathering. Within minutes, the chairman and the committees were in place. "Our goal is to have the most spectacular Christmas party the church has ever had." The committee met once or twice a week from that night on in a frenzy of activity. A catering service and full-blown orchestra were retained. The great social hall was finally turned into a gala ball room. Fountains of water sprayed upward through colored lights from the center of the room. Artificial trees and screens gave setting for the tables. The program, which I've forgotten by now, did last until midnight. There was little to remind one that this was a church function. It just wasn't possible to get into the true spirit of Christmas that year.

I must say money was not a problem. My salary was the highest it had been of all my years of pastoring. A wealthy member's son, also a minister, was sent to tell me that my pulpit relations were excellent. He let me know that I would not lack for money if I maintained my present performance. There was just one thing I must be aware of. Don't ding the congregation about prayer meetings or old fashioned holiness. A one hundred thousand dollar endowment policy was being considered which the church would pay out in five years, and it would be mine if things went well. A West Coast daily radio broadcast on one of Seattle's fifty thousand watt stations was promised me. A generous housing allowance was already in place plus an ample auto expense account. I was in a substantial place financially, not to mention the Northwest College salary as well. Only the sick feeling in the pit of my stomach bode ill to the whole deal. I now understood why no more than a half dozen souls beside my wife and me ever attended the twice weekly morning prayer meeting. It became obvious that social life in the church easily outweighed spiritual life. This was the state of affairs on a rainy Sunday night, as Margie, my family and I made our way to a social gathering in Seattle's Ballard District.

Several prominent church families had invited us after service to join them for an evening of fellowship and food. The expectation of our presence was so strong, we didn't think it wise to decline. The accident that totally changed my life took less than five seconds to unfold. The windshield wipers quietly sweeping back the rain joined the soft chatter of our children as we approached the blind intersection, where the accident occurred. It was as if Fate had arranged all the details. The approaching lights to the left of our Buick station wagon kept right on coming, even though we had the right of way. First the gentle, then jarring crash just in front of the door on my side, my split second "Hang on!" and I turned my head away from the glass that didn't explode. The offending automobile had actually followed us as we cleared the intersection in order to strike our wagon's front left corner. No one seemed hurt other than our bent front bumper and fender which was creased up against the tire. I attributed my sense of nausea to the cold night and slight excitement the relatively minor incident had caused. My neck and shoulder muscles seemed a bit tense.

"Fifth accident on this corner this year," the owner of the elevated home on the far corner proclaimed. "Wonder when the city is going to do something to make this street safer." The small man who was driver of the auto that hit us, seemed totally confused. I thought him to be acting as one who might be under the influence of alcohol. The police wouldn't come, "No injuries," they explained. The small man's car suffered no damage. His oversized front bumper did all the mayhem to our crumpled front fender. Our fender was pried back from the tire by the helpful far corner house owner. Margie and the children were by now within the hospitable warmth of the kind people's home. We chose to continue on to the food and fun gathering but were able to beg our way out within a few moments due to the accident. Something began that dark rainy Sunday night, that would extricate me from the prison house of my own dreams, as surely as a successful jail break.

  My bondage was deeper than the church and congregation I was pastoring. It was as if I was breaking out to freedom from deep within enemy territory. The strange truth was, these were no enemies. After the accident, my neck and shoulders continued to ache and give me pain. A Seventh Day Adventist doctor was recommended and within the week, I found my way to his office. "Whiplash, Reverend," I was told by the pleasant medical examiner. "You'll need bed rest, maybe traction." "Wait a minute, Dr. Allen," I objected! "You sound like my mother. The truth is I've got no time to rest, let alone stop for traction." "You preachers are all alike," I was informed. "Just remember that you are seriously injured, and you will be back!" To humor Dr. Allen, I agreed to wear an awkward plastic neck brace home.

  I did manage to last part way through the Sunday morning service two days later before nearly passing out in the pulpit. My song leader took the closing of the meeting and I slipped back to my office and slumped into my chair in pain. Margie read the situation and came to me minutes later. We called Dr. Allen who agreed to meet at Seattle's North Gate Hospital. Within days, I could see that this situation was beyond my control. Examination and x-rays showed injury to several upper neck disks. When I had turned my head to avoid possible flying glass in the bumper car incident, the sharp jolt had popped my head forward and back, causing the injury. Until that moment, I had thought that whiplash was an invention of lawyers, to milk insurance companies from some of their surplus profit. The church was mildly concerned, mainly wanting to know when I'd be out of the hospital and back on duty. The college rolled with the punches, and substituted for my classes. Traction came next, a whole month of it! The whole thing was almost ridiculous. I felt like a fish that found itself high and dry with no way to get back into the water. The worst was yet to follow. Traction did not relieve the numbness in my hands. The neck and shoulder pain continued. A neurosurgeon was brought in and surgery was recommended. I worried about Margie and the children, but was told by my wife that everyone was doing great. Broken bones was one thing everyone could understand, but injury to tissue and nerves was harder to verify.

The night before surgery, Dr. Allen and the neurosurgeon appeared at the foot of my bed for a final conference. Some conference! "Well, Reverend, how does it feel to be in the bed, facing surgery, rather than by the bedside giving comfort? How do you feel about tomorrow?" My answer sent the two away grinning. "I'm not just depending on you two tomorrow," I told them, "I'm praying God will help in the surgery." Four and one half hours were needed the next day to perform the laminectomy on my neck. My wife was waiting for me by the green double doors to come out of surgery. I was rolled by, whiter than the sheet I was wrapped in and pasty looking besides. "Looks good doesn't he?" the Seventh Day Adventist doctor lied.

I came slowly to the surface of consciousness in the recovery room. The first sense I became aware of was a painful throb at the base of my skull. My neck felt as if it was pressed onto the sharp corners of a brick. "I want to turn," I croaked to the special nurse. "Sorry, Reverend," I was told, "you will need to lie in this position for two more days." This kind of pain was brand new to me. My left arm felt limp. I was given a shot and the burning in my neck resided.

A dream came during the next night, after Margie left me. I seemed to be at the church. Some kind of a party was in progress. "It will be fun, Pastor, you need to loosen up and have a good time." These men, some of them officers in the Assembly, wanted me to strip off my shirt and let them apply body paint. There was a slide that went downward and into the church basement. It was their intention to send me down the slide after painting me. I seemed to cause a great disappointment when I refused to comply to the wishes of the men. I remembered the dream the next morning and told Margie the only description I could use to describe the experience was "Mardi Gras."

    Healthy patients recover from a surgery like the one I underwent in relatively short time. I did not! I seemed to be caught in quick sand. I didn't sink, but just couldn't get out. A second dream came a few nights later. I found myself in the interior of a cement silo. There were very high cement walls all around me. There were no doors or windows. I knew I was hopelessly trapped within the walls. Suddenly, to my great surprise, an opening about one foot wide began appearing at the top of the cement wall and came downward to the floor in front of me. "Go through the opening," I heard a clear voice speak. Looking out through the narrow space, I saw only blue sky.

    I just wasn't able to gain strength or weight. By now my weight was down to what I weighed in junior high school, one hundred forty-eight pounds. I could not walk without much help. There was very little resemblance to my usual healthy one hundred eighty pound self. My left arm hung useless by my side. Walking would have to be learned again. There was no way I could return to either the church or college job in the near future. Margie and I talked at length on one of her visits, as to our best options in light of our circumstances. We came to a simple conclusion. The only thing we could do was to resign from the church pastorate. No way would they be willing to wait a possible year for my full recovery. Nor did we expect them to! On Margie's next visit we wrote up the resignation, my wife had it typed, and I signed. The letter was accepted by the church board, reluctantly of course, and I slid out the narrow opening of my cement silo prison, sideways, into bright blue sky. After two and one half months and nearly twenty thousand dollars in hospital bills, I checked out, and went home to Lake Forest Park.

In an escape, one is not free just because he breaks out of a jail! There is much more to obtaining freedom than that. Gulliver of Gulliver's Travels had hundreds of tiny ropes holding him to the ground. Each binding must be individually broken. What would I do with a shattered dream? Broken health had number one priority. We had the future to consider, debts to be dealt with and broken pieces of life to tie back together.

No person has the slightest clue as to their true character until they go through a major crisis. The weight of men's value systems and integrity can be measured at such a time. D.V. Hurst, the Northwest College President, simply took my not being able to continue teaching my classes in stride. He saw to my being paid to the end of my contract. My brief relationship with the man was very refreshing. The financial chairman at the church held another view of the matter. "Don't work, don't eat; or, if you don't preach, don't reach for your pay check." Others prevailed on our behalf and we didn't have to do as was suggested – pay back my salary given us while I was in the hospital. My church office secretary came by the house to see me, and came close to violating our unspoken agreement. She carefully worked around the question as to the absolute necessity of my resignation. There was a shadow of doubt somewhere in the depths of her blue eyes. I never cleared up the issue for her.

The insurance companies wouldn't pay, neither the man's who caused the accident, or my own company, so I sought advise from a lawyer. The hospital, doctors, related individuals including my physical therapist, all wanted to be paid – a very reasonable request. A court trial became necessary. I became the plaintiff, and the little man who drove the vehicle that hit me, the defendant. Court is an impressive place. The whole procedure a bit beyond the uninitiated. I obtained my attorney from a law firm recommended by friends. Their offices were located in what had been at one time a land mark in south Seattle, now dwarfed and squat appearing. The tower was not far from the King Dome. The lawyer I was assigned to did not have his name in gold print on the appointment room doors. Melvin Beli or Perry Mason he was not. In the courtroom he was towered over by the defense's council. The case was actually decided within minutes of the defense's opening arguments. The jury was chosen, the plaintiff's case carefully laid out, when the deciding moment of drama occurred that sent Margie and me home with no settlement. The trial actually continued for several days but was really settled within minutes of the defense's first move. The defense attorney placed the nervous little defendant on the stand and began to ask him routine questions. Without warning or apparent reason, the man who caused the accident broke out in a loud cry almost sobbing. "Please don't send me to jail!" he pleaded. "Please! Please!" The entire court room gasped in shock. The newly appointed jury reeled in puzzled concern. The case was settled. Facts played no part in the outcome after this. The preacher, whose task in life is to give comfort to the poor and needy, was agent in bringing great distress to a poor hapless fellow – no matter if my vehicle had the right of way. The fact that the other driver could have driven straight through the intersection without hitting us, if he hadn't swerved two car lengths to his left, didn't count. Even the judge's instructions made it clear that I was not at fault. The jury was to determine the extent of damages.

    I watched the defense attorney while everyone else was in shock and puzzlement. His pleasure was obvious as the judge called a recess to quiet the little man. The defense knew he had scored a major hit on his opening shot. As the trial ended, while our losing attorney gathered up his papers, Margie and I stood looking out upon the dreary wet scene below the courtroom window. "We'll ask for retrial," our council stated as he left. The judge did tell the jury he was going to consider tossing out their verdict.

    "Mr. and Mrs. Clarke," a voice behind us called softly. We both recognized the speaker at once – the lawyer who defended the dangerous little driver. "I hope you'll believe me when I say I'm truly sorry for you." Margie and I turned slowly, questioning if we were hearing right. The smooth talking attorney continued. "I really felt you deserved a decent settlement. You know, I did offer your attorney $30,000 after the first session." We did know, but were not given a chance to accept. "You bet!" our council had told us, "they'll be offering a lot more before I get through with them!" It was strange to have our comfort come from the opposing lawyer. The truth was, he didn't have to say anything. The judge did throw out the jury's decision, and another trial date was set. Our case was then back in a better position. Negotiation began with the insurance company and a settlement was reached out of court. The outcome paid all our bills with a few thousand left to carry my family during the next few months of my recuperation. I did a bit of dealing with our attorney to reduce his share of the settlement take. My argument was simple. Since my attorney was unsuccessful in court, and the insurance company had already offered thirty thousand dollars, close to what we settled for, what had he earned? This logic prevailed and we came out nearly as well as if we had won in the courtroom. The great item not paid for in all my sufferings was the pain I went through. There was a benefiting factor money could not buy, however – my escape!

One final dream came, showing me a dimension of my release from the church in most drastic full drama. In the dream, I was riding in a police vehicle next to the driver. The policeman was driving through an area similar to that of the church I had been pastoring. Suddenly, as we approached an intersection, several cars entered the intersection from every direction, smashing into each other. Accidents seemed to happen almost everywhere on the streets. The most spectacular crash was when two or three cars plowed into a passing train. The train was making a great noise as it came by. The cars actually began to give off a great fireworks as they hit the train, spewing sparks and fire everywhere. I turned to the policeman to ask him why all of this was happening. "Don't you see?" the officer asked me. "They've taken down all the traffic signs and signals." I looked quickly around to see where signs are normally placed, and true to the policeman's word, there were no traffic signs anywhere.

The restraints had been removed! Strange and ironic, the pastor who followed me in the church conducted 22 funeral services in the next 24 month period. The dream I had had, seemed in some way related to the bizarre chain of deaths. When I failed to improve physically over the next few weeks, my Seventh Day Adventist doctor recommended that I seek aid from the social security program. At first, this seemed an unthinkable thing for me to even consider. I had helped the people in the church get welfare help. I just never considered I was the kind who qualified. My former church secretary and husband came by on another kind of visit, and when the subject came up, got onto my case rather strongly. "Pastor Clarke, social security isn't welfare!" she told me. "Social security is insurance for just such cases as yours. You get down there, and obtain the help you need." A few days later, Margie and I found ourselves in the nearest social security office with an appointment number in our hand. The interview wasn't as bad as I expected. I left the office with an appointment to see a government medical examiner a few days later. Have no fear, the government doctors don't just declare anyone disabled. The tests I was put through were complete and I had no clue whether I had done well or poorly. "You will be notified of the results," was all we were told. A few weeks later, a fat official letter came from the social security insurance department in Philadelphia, notifying me that I had been declared totally disabled. Checks began coming at about the same time. This was like a man treading water having a row boat shoved up close where he could climb in and paddle to shore.

God seemed to step forward from out of the shadows. He didn't heal me at once, as he had done so often before. Nor did all my problems dissolve immediately. I was like a bird with a mending crippled wing, faintly conscious that flight into the blue sky beyond my prison was possible. Several happenings were of definite Divine origin. First, twenty-five hundred dollars appeared mysteriously in our bank account. Those most likely responsible strongly denied any involvement. Then one day, trucks carrying a load of carpet backed up to the front door of our unfinished remodeled house. I stumbled out through the front door, dragging my left leg to chase the carpet installers away. "Wrong address," I called out. "We didn't order any carpet, no money!" "Mr. Clarke, we have the right house, the carpet is paid for, we do need to get started!" As Margie came out to join me in my astonishment, the men began carrying in rolls of beautiful carpet. John Mark joined quickly to help. Hanging on to the rolls, he was dragged along from room to room as the workmen distributed the floor covering. The colors, the thick shag, the sizes! Who? When did all this get decided? By the time the girls: Beth, Lynn, and Marliss arrived from school, the living room, Beth's room and dining areas were carpeted. The old worn carpets were outside to be carried away. What a joy the carpet was during my recovery, a daily reminder of love and care. The carpet puzzle was solved when Chick and Dorothy Kravagna came forward to confess to the carpet caper. Owners of a Lynwood furniture store, both had been in our home and had appreciated our ministry in the church.

In late summer a phone call came in, carrying a very surprising proposal. Margie and I were invited to picturesque Couer d'Alene, Idaho to become pastors at the First Assembly there. Everyone in the northwest district had heard of my accident and poor physical condition. Why did the Couer d'Alene church wish to consider having me come to something I was in no condition to perform? With that call and the letter of invitation that followed, something like a gentle breeze from heaven swept over me. I had been told by the medical people I would never be able to pastor again. Nerves injured as severely as mine had been, would never fully heal. My brother Neal had suffered a similar injury and had continued to suffer greatly for many years after his jolting accident.

God's finger at work in my affairs, regardless if I would be able to accept the Couer d'Alene offer or not, brought an infusion of hope. Not the shouting kind of hope, but rather a smoldering slow igniting kind of a spark of promise. I stood like a man blind from years of being away from the bright light, beginning the painful task of focusing his eyes in the brilliance of the sun. A transformation was beginning to quietly stir within me, one that would take several years to fully emerge.

The book "Long Walk" is a most extraordinary escape account of prisoners in a barbaric Siberian Soviet spring camp. Breaking out through the barbed wire on a heavily snowing early spring night was only the most minor part of their heroic saga. Choosing an unexpected and impossible direction of flight, the escapees fled southward in a state of semi starvation. Five men crossed a burning desert and impossible mountains, and eventually gained liberty. Then the prisoners faced something only a few were able to live through. The momentum that carried them during their escape was not adequate to help them survive their new freedom. The prisoners, after years of extremely cruel unjustified interment, had no way to prepare to endure the great trauma of their new life beyond barbed wire. It is said that there are those who choose to remain in their sordid state of life and bondage rather than face the rigors of change and the challenge that liberation would require.

You may wonder how just a few months of pain and total disruption of routine could have had such a drastic affect on me. Just as no two people respond uniformly to a stimulus or electric shock, neither do all individuals react the same in a given crisis. My crisis seemed tailor-made to start my life in a completely new direction. I would not be going to Couer d'Alene as pastor because I was obviously the best candidate they could have picked. When everything worked out and Margie and I felt to accept the offer, I knew either God had something to do with the decision, or the church was extremely benevolent, or just a little nutty.

Spring ended with a dramatic note that year. Our daughter Beth and Glen, an engineering graduate of the University of Washington, who had been acquaintances and friends for many years, decided to save Margie and me the cost of an expensive church wedding. They eloped and married in a small town nearby. After the shock and disappointment passed, our relationship reestablished itself. It became evident the choice was right and a marvelous marriage came out of the union. Margie and I could never have wished for a better providing, caring, godly husband for Beth than Glen has turned out to be.

The Boeing airplane manufacturers chose this exact time to take a financial nose dive. When Boeing, a major factor in the greater Seattle economy, caught a cold, the rest of the business community got pneumonia! Real estate stagnated, so we could not dispose of our Lake Forest Park property. I did fly to Couer d'Alene, Idaho, taking four-year-old John Mark with me, to check out the church to see if they really knew what they were asking for. Even though I spent most of the visit resting at one of the homes and only gave a short sermon, everyone seemed satisfied. I really think it was John Mark's behavior that clinched the deal for us. John displayed a remarkable act of endurance during the visit. During the service, he sat like a tin soldier on the front row. My short sermon on the wonders of heaven and why I believed it wasn't far "beyond the stars" won me acclaim for sure from one board member. In late summer we rented out the secluded hilltop house in Lake Forest Park and moved to beautiful Couer d'Alene, Idaho. Leaving Seattle and the Northend Church and the college job put distance between me and the scene of my ungraceful escape. The move taught me an extraordinary lesson. A dream and ambition does not die an easy death. My time in Couer d'Alene would prove this to me.

The cross state drive was easy. The snow-capped Cascade mountains, guarding the excellent Snoqualmie Pass, gave way to the fruitful Kittitas Valley. Next came the volcanic transformation between the moonlike landscape beyond the valley and the vast Columbia Basin. Don't question the amazing contrast Washington State boasts about! It lays across the four hundred miles like a grand design in variety. In our truck with our household things and Buick station wagon we passed through Spokane and on into Idaho's narrow panhandle country. One of the world's most beautiful lakes can be seen as traffic approaches the lovely city whose name means, "In the Heart of Eleanor." The Couer d'Alene Assembly turned out to be just as they appeared, very benevolent – in my case this meant easy going, considerate, and generous. Several other things contributed to my recovery. There just wasn't any pressure. Margie and the children settled in quickly. Deep in my spirit, a message came that I was back home. Childhood roots took nourishment and grew. Years of faithful physical conditioning paid off. My body and nerves responded and somewhere in those early months in Couer d'Alene, my positive optimistic and upbeat spirit bobbed back up to the surface. I found myself ready for action again.

A little over two years after being declared totally disabled, I was ready to go off of the disability provision. It wasn't that simple. The government doesn't declare you totally disabled for life, and then two and a half years later, let you waltz in and say, "Oh by the way, I'm just fine now." The government just doesn't have a form to fill out where you check a space that reads, "God performed a miracle; I'm now healed, don't send any more money." As the checks came, I sent them back. My philosophy was that I since didn't need the help, they should give it to someone who did. The Assembly was providing housing and a salary and the social security insurance had served its purpose. Finally the checks stopped coming. Shortly afterward, however, a letter arrived from the department that defied my imagination. The letter read, "Since you are well now, and don't need the benefits, obviously you never were in need of them. Please send all the money back that you have received." I took the letter to the local office and left in a state of great bafflement. I now owed the United States Government thousands of dollars. The local social security office somehow arranged a hearing for me with an independent federal judge. I drove to Spokane by myself on the day of the hearing. The building was large and intimidating. I took the elevator to the floor designated, and entered a huge room. Nearly empty, its only furnishing was a desk-like table in the middle of the room, two chairs in front of it, a U.S. flag, and a bench by the front door where I seated myself. A secretary entered from a door in the back and let me know I was in the right place. The judge would be out shortly. All business, the impressive appearing federal arbitrator came quickly to the table, invited me to be seated and seated himself. "Now, Mr. Clarke," he began, "don't be nervous, I don't work for the social security people. I'm here to give you a fair hearing. My word will be final in this case." I think I was encouraged, so I started at the beginning and gave my account of the matter. When I finished, the judge shook his head and said, "I can see why you are a bit bewildered at the turn of events. Go home, don't worry, I'll fix this thing up for you." The federal arbitrator did just as he promised. In the last mail before Christmas that year, I received an official letter clearing me of any wrong doing. The social security insurance office, who issued the letter demanding repayment, was declared ludicrous in their request.

    Getting out of that problem freed me to get into another one. I've always considered people who don't learn the first time to be slow learners. I would have to fit in this category. In going to Seattle and playing out the full drama of my misguided fantasy of success, I hadn't fully escaped. It took an event just short of a broken neck to extricate me from the dilemma of my own doing in the queen city. This next time, only a true escape into reality would set me on the road to freedom.

Escape is really an ongoing thing. Life continues to weave a web of circumstances and situations from which we all seek exodus. It's not strange that the Bible devotes several books describing and chronicling the escape of His people out of ancient Egypt. Not too much has changed. The memory has such a short span. For Israel of old, the day came when the former bondage in Egypt looked better than the present price of final freedom. To those people described in Exodus, the past with its misery seemed to fade away, and a picture of absolute unreality took its place. In my case, I was simply blind. I could not see what God was trying to deliver me from – not circumstances and ever-changing situations, but from the product of my own deception, my view of success and fulfillment.

Each person's first attempt at escape is from that over which they had no control – their origin, their roots, and what they were born to. The second attempt, if they are fortunate enough to discover their imprisonment, is from what they have become. The rewards of hard years of arriving are often too sweet to cast aside very easily. Jesus must have been referring to this when he said, "Not many great, mighty or really rich shall be saved." I know what he meant by being saved. He meant it would be extremely difficult for these to be saved from themselves. No one casts a hard-earned dream aside so lightly. Escape in its true and final form is not from something; escape is really a passage into something. That something we must escape into is called reality. My flight to freedom had yet one more journey – through the hall of mirrors, into the great room of discovery.

To be able to face the truth about ourselves, assuming full responsibility for our actions, finally seeing things as they really are and being willing to change at whatever cost, seems to be a good start toward finding reality.

Hebrews 2:3 (KJV)

How shall we escape if we neglect so great salvation; which at first began to be spoken by the Lord, and was confirmed unto us by them that heard him.

CHAPTER TWELVE

INTO REALITY

The road to reality is down the proper paths of thought. Our own unguarded and untutored ways of thinking will never lead us into the golden realm of reality. Only a profound miracle of God will bring us into that grand room of discovery. But we must first walk the hallway of mirrors. Here, we at last can see ourselves as we really are. We will see ourselves as we were, as what we have become, and as what we must yet be. We now are what we have been. We shall become what we now are. Only a dramatic change is adequate to break the inevitable chain. Divine intervention is our only hope for escape into reality.

How did I escape? It was not easy. Picture a man blindfolded, walking along in a deep trench on a one-way road, and you have the first view of me in the hall of mirrors. I dwelt in a state of certainty that the work I did for God was all that counted. Again, I was ready to plunge into another great endeavor to build something very substantial for God's Kingdom. Never mind that an act of God just short of breaking my neck got me out of my last plan of accomplishment. Being a believing Christian is not something we do, it is something we are. The great godly acts of church history were accomplished by those who first became, and then acted. The reality of all of this had not yet broken across my understanding.

After my divinely aided recovery, I happily plunged into a full scale of activity. Before another year had passed, I became a member of the Couer d'Alene Kiwanis Service Club, President of the neighborhood P.T.A., and the presbyter of some thirty greater Spokane area assemblies. The church grew during this time, and a second Sunday morning service was added.

Several things triggered a fresh and exciting turn in my ministry – the concept of mother churches sponsoring home-mission kinds of outreach. The Evangel, the National Assemblies publication, carried an article where the mother church – rather than expanding its present facilities – actually sent out six or seven families to start a new assembly in the nearby area. In one case the pastor resigned and went to help the new assembly get started, certainly a wonderful concept in pioneering a new church. The idea was quickened to me. I slowly and carefully examined the idea with the local church board and district officials. A year later, after obtaining total support for the idea at the annual church business meeting, approval was given to the proposal. The plan called for no more than seven families and myself to start the second Couer d'Alene Assembly. I would resign, allowing the Mother Church ample time to select a new pastor, and more time for him to become fully settled in before starting any kind of new church meeting activities or advertising. I resigned and obtained a teaching job in the local mid-high school in order to support my family in this exciting new venture.

Usually, new small church works had a young pastor new at the business. It made tremendous sense for someone like me, with a great deal of experience to pioneer such an attempt at expansion. The Mother Church became tardy in finding a new pastor. This delay would eventually flaw the carefully planned and executed new growth attempt. Word of this came to me while attending the General Council gathering held in Kansas City. Some of the Mother Church board members had contacted my district superintendent to express concern over the new outreach. "Pastor Clarke will create too much competition for the Mother Church," was their concern. I held the idea that we all were on the same team. By this time, six months had passed. The small nucleus had rented the Seventh Day Adventist's gymnasium and set an approaching date for the kick-off services.

On the day the new church opened its doors for the first time, our family decided to guess how many people might show up. I, of course, had counted all heads who had said they would be there and added a scriptural ten percent. Numbers guessed by Margie and the girls ranged from 50-75. At this point, John Mark spoke up stating that he had hopes for "better things." His estimate was that 110 would be there! He had one other contribution to add – "we shouldn't call the new group People's Church, it should be called 'People's Cathedral.'" Actually, John Mark's view was a bit bodacious in light of the fact that no newspaper advertisement had been issued, only word of mouth to the families selected for the project. But he certainly was not lacking in faith and vision.

My first knowledge of a serious problem came shortly after our first few services had been conducted. The thrill of over 100 in attendance on opening day carried me through the shock of a phone call from the district office requesting me to shut down the new church and return to the Mother Church and resume pastoring there. I must admit that I failed to see any reality in the strong suggestion. If the Mother Church had a concern, I had a problem! To abandon the families involved in the project, plus dozens of people attracted to the appeal of a new beginning, was asking more than my conscience would allow me to do. Next I was informed that the new church could not be called Assembly Number Two. Finally, after meeting with the district presbytery, of which I was a member, I was told that my credentials could be in jeopardy. My blend of sanguine, melancholic, choleric, and phlegmatic personality carried me through all this with only a couple of statements in question. Why had my friend, the district superintendent who had agreed with me, changed his mind, and why did the Mother Church wait for months before expressing any concern?

Margie was troubled by the change of position of our previous board and district officials. The statement by my friend, the superintendent, that "We always side with the Mother Church," didn't satisfy her view of fairness or integrity. Margie's sweet and gentle spirit was troubled by the position I was placed in due to the reversal. During her years of nurturing and peace-making, she had come to see strife and contention as the greatest enemies of the church. A new reality was growing from my life's experience. Nothing happens outside of God's purpose for those given to His will. I was later asked, "Who do you blame for all this?" To their surprise I answered, "No one. Somehow God is in it all."

The new work was named the People's Church, and my credentials simply lapsed due to lack of application for renewal.

One year later the Easter attendance of both the Mother Church and the orphaned new group totaled nearly twice what the Mother Church had a year earlier. I did not see myself as oppressed in all that had occurred, only challenged to keep my heart right in it all.

Meeting a wealthy local land owner was the second factor in the continuing momentum of my new thrust. Thirty acres on the freeway between two key exits was probably the most exciting property available at the time. It turned out that my new millionaire friend owned the property. After adds were placed in the local press announcing the new concept of a church without walls, I received a call from the owner of the coveted 30 acres of rolling timber-covered property by the freeway.

"Reverend Clarke," the owner told me, "I would consider selling the acreage to you for your new church." Neither price nor terms were mentioned at the time, but this appeared to be an incredible opportunity for Peoples' Church. The church board and congregation was in a "go" mode. I was given the go-ahead to see what kind of terms we could get. After a couple of meetings with the land owner this was the agreement: Price $150,000. Terms: deferred payments for five years. Such a deal is totally unheard of. One large lot on the corner of the freeway exit sold by the same man for $200,000 cash. My conclusion was that only God could cause an astute businessman to sell so much land at such an extraordinary price!

Next came the architect, a man with a flare for the daring. The church sent me the architect, and another board member to California to study unusual church structures, and bring home some ideas. The Robert Schuller glass cathedral certainly required a visit; Melody Land and several other contemporary churches drew us to view their plans. We attended a Schuller seminar on church growth, and came under the drawing of his magnetic personality. After a special breakfast together with Robert Schuller, where the three of us outlined some ideas for People's Church, he promised to tutor our project.

Back in Couer d'Alene, we went into action. Our concept for what would eventually become "People's Cathedral" had a wide range of adaptation. A drive-in church, a 100-foot high wedding chapel, plus elevators and escalators were only a few of the special features of our plan. We did decline an all-glass structure like the Schuller church in Garden Grove, California as being a bit far out for North Idaho. We decided to build a multipurpose building first. My engineer son-in-law began laying out the lot for the first unit. Doug Cranston, the architect, produced a model and prints of the church plan. All we lacked was money, lots of money. There was no shortage of enthusiasm, and the congregation was growing. None of us thought lack of funds was going to be a problem.

The beginning of Margie's health problems seemed minor at first. Our naturopath doctor and the M.D. we visited were not too concerned. We took a lengthy vacation that summer. Our travels ranged along the Oregon coast south to Disney Land and Newport Beach in California. A visit to Knox Berry Farm closed out our time in the golden state. Newport Beach drew us to the sun and surf. I walked for a mile or more down the beach from where Margie and the children had set up their area of activity in the sand and rays of Ole Sol. Time receded as I turned back toward the tiny dots I knew were my family. As I approached the sand castles the children had made, I noticed Margie was asleep under the slightly overcast heat of the sun. When I woke Margie, I was surprised to discover she had been lying quietly in the warm blaze for over an hour while I was gone. The dull red was already beginning to show on her exposed limbs and back. Margie developed a severe case of sunburn. Her misery from the burn and blistering for several days was sad to behold. There was no question that the severe sunburn taxed Margie's lymph system.

We did cross the corner of New Mexico driving through Las Vegas on our way to the Grand Canyon. I headed our Buick station wagon homeward, stopping briefly at Salt Lake City. The cool mountains of Idaho welcomed us back to the great northwest. At home in Couer d'Alene, a current of preschool activities swept us all out of our vacation wagon into the full force of our busy lives. I took Margie to be checked out by first the naturopath, and then the M.D. A small growth was detected in her abdomen.

My teaching position at the mid high school required most of my time for the next several days. Margie seemed well and able to step into the school days pace. In mid-September I took Margie to a faculty dinner for teachers and their spouses of the mid high school. Part way through the evening Margie said she wasn't feeling well, so I took her home.

Margie had always been extremely healthy, and an Adelle Davis health care follower. No one, including me, worried about Margie's condition. To be safe, I scheduled an appointment for Margie at the Spokane Rockwood Clinic. The reports were good, showing my wife to be in basic good health. We were told to watch the swelling in her stomach area which the examiner said may have been stirred up by the serious case of sunburn. There was, of course, no direct connection between the sunburn and the abdominal swelling, only the burden on Margie's lymph system affected her body's ability to wage war on the intruder in Margie's abdomen.

The weeks flew by as our family and church prayed and believed for Margie's return to full health and vigor. No doctor recommended radical treatment or surgery. This was a great relief to my wife. Margie's faith was absolute, her testimony simple. "God will completely heal me. If he doesn't, I will not put my trust in anyone else." Margie made me promise that if her condition somehow worsened, under no circumstance was I to take her into the hospital for a last flurry of treatments. Such a promise is most difficult to agree to keep. I wanted to do everything possible to insure my wife's recovery, short of violating her great faith. If anyone thought we should have done more, they never voiced it. I could see Margie very gradually losing strength and weight.

Christmas came with my wife well enough to enter in and take an active part in the festivities. Her Christmas card to me expressed her great thankfulness to the Lord and to me for a lifetime of happiness. "I cannot think of a single thing or joy I could ever desire," was Margie's message on that special card. "I feel completely fulfilled," she concluded. These penned words were to become a source of great comfort to me.

Margie's condition did not improve. Days were spent on her bed with Margie reading and praying and enjoying anyone who came by to visit. Our children were always nearby to help. Beth came to add her strength and the children's Aunt Marie came to add her prayers and faith. John Mark spent many afternoons quietly playing and talking to his mom on the corner of our great king sized bed. None of us had any doubt at all but that prayer and faith would prevail! Margie would get well!

An early Saturday morning in February Margie went out to lunch with some women from the church. The following week was spent quietly at home enjoying the newly re-carpeted house, a pre-Christmas improvement. Margie stayed at home the next Sunday morning saying she would be just fine. I found Margie in a state of excitement when I arrived after the service. "It's all settled," my wife told me. "Everything is going to be okay." When asked to explain, Margie said the Lord had spoken to her and given her a promise. She showed me some scriptures in Hosea chapter 6 verses 7 and 8. "He hath torn, He will heal us ...After two days will He revive us: In the third day He will raise us up..." I was lifted by Margie's excitement. We had a wonderful time around the dinner table, as our family all believed the battle had been won.

At midnight that evening Margie took a turn for the worse and by morning she was greatly weakened. Marie stayed with Margie and me through the night. The new day brought a rally and we all relaxed a little. Of course, the church and family were alerted to keep praying. Tuesday dawned with little change. We all knew the third day was coming and our test of faith would be over. I slept fitfully off and on Tuesday night, mostly in a state of alertness. That February morning came grey and cold. At 6:00 a.m. Margie called me and we talked for nearly an hour. The children all came in before school to see their mother. Marie and I felt they should go on to school even though it was obvious my wife was in a weakened condition. One hour later I came to Margie's side of our bed and took her in my arms. "How are you doing?" I asked her. I was given a weak smile in response. Margie then told me that it was hard for her to live in a world where people in the country and church failed to live in the kind of peace God intended them to live in. My dear wife relaxed in my arms and seemed to drift into a gentle sleep. I called her name at first quietly, then louder. There was no response. I did not recognize or accept that this could be death. Laying Margie's head back carefully onto her pillow, I called up the stairs for Marie then I called out to Margie in absolute faith, "Awaken! In the name of Jesus!" If she had died, by faith I would raise her from the dead. After the doctor came and pronounced Margie dead, I was forced to slowly accept the truth – she was now a resident in the realm where everyone lived together in a state of great peace, in the kind of peace she had just stated it was hard for her to live without.

Numbness came bringing a merciful dullness to the indescribable pain of my loss. The quiet shadowy movements of family and friends carried out the necessary administrations of the moment. Facing death is life's strongest reality. Several times in my life I had faced the danger of my own dying. Mother, Father, a sister I had never seen, and a four-year-old brother had made passage through the veil to the land beyond our view, but the full reality of dying had never hit me. I had also stood by dozens of grave sides and ministered to grieving relatives. The unreal facade and mastery of funeral homes almost totally masked death's grim face. Now I had watched as the precious light of life flicked out in Margie's lovely face. Her eyes closed to this earthly scene, and the vital strength and force of my wife's being flowed into the river called eternity. We were left alone on the shores of time, while my wife and the children's mother sailed away out of sight beyond our horizon.

"Our largest funeral that I can remember," the director of the home whispered to me. The statement was intended to be of comfort to me. I rather saw the sizable crowd waiting in the chapel as more of a tribute to Margie. This grey February day had started early for me. Before dawn I had settled in the quietness of the family room seeking special inner strength to face the full reality of this day – full and final temporal separation from Margie. The Bible in my lap lay opened to the 110th Psalm. I can say I was impressed to turn to these verses. Of all the possible Psalms I could have turned to, this Psalm was certainly more veiled in meaning to me at the time than most.

Yet a comfort sprang from some well in the Spirit. The words "Thy strength out of Zion, and rule in the midst of thy enemies," coupled with "Thou hast the dew of thy youth..." sustained me, and I left that quiet time an hour later knowing I could face the hours ahead of me.

Margie had always been emphatic about one aspect of funerals she didn't like – opening the casket and having people file past and stare down at the deceased. "I sure don't want that at my funeral," was always Margie's summation of her view on the matter. "Why look at the person when they are not really there?" I requested that viewing of Margie be done at the funeral home. Her casket would not be opened at the memorial service. Our family did one other thing on the day of the funeral that I had never seen done before. We all elected to walk in at the time my wife's casket was brought in. After this moment, the next two hours blended together in quiet shades of memory – kind and comforting words, close warm presences of family and friends, and the final moments at the grave side in view of the nearby North Idaho mountains.

A new reality came to me that day, hope of "life" beyond life. We had not only faced death in my wife's departure, but also the hope of life beyond earth's brief span. The full weight of that so called "Blessed Hope" only comes when you lose someone so dear. A seal is broken, opening a new vista, a view into eternity and a place where earthly treasures are placed, safe, beyond time! After Margie's funeral, everything seemed to stop for nearly a year. The mid-high gave me a one month leave of absence. I had someone else fill in at the church for two weeks. All thought of the church building project was cast out of my mind. It was as if a hand had reached down inside of my chest, grabbed a handfull of delicate wiring and pulled it out. I felt totally disconnected. My children, the church, and the mid-high school teaching position did, however, give me reason to function. Without Margie the days held less substance and purpose. It was like losing the navigator on an air flight requiring instruments. Direction was no longer in focus. I had to regain a new capacity to face the future. I needed a new reality, a deep and enduring reason for what I now should be doing.

This reality did not come at once. Within months it would. The weeks did fly by. Classes at the mid-high came and went. The church managed nicely and spring arrived warm and green in a bathing of new promise. When school lets out, I promised myself, I would get away for a few weeks and view everything from a perspective removed enough to allow objectivity. I chose Hawaii, the pacific paradise, 2,000 miles west of Los Angeles. My children would go with me including Beth. We would stay at least a month. Good advice was received from a former island dweller – skip the tours, find your own hotel four or five blocks from the beach, prices are very reasonable. So we found all this to be true. In the Honolulu airport we all huddled for rehearsal of our plan. We took the bus to the Wakiki area and dumped our luggage at the bus stop side walk. The girls guarded it while I scouted out and secured hotel accommodations. Within an hour we were tucked in. The girls in bathing suits were on their way to Wakiki under the shadow of Honolulu's famous Diamond Head. Within hours, white skin turned pink. A young friend of daughter Lynn, who had practically stowed away in order to make the trip, became so sun burned it was necessary to call her parents and put her on a flight back to Seattle. Her trip of a lifetime lasted only three days. Thus warned of the dangers of the sun's rays, Beth, Lynn and Marliss took a more cautious approach, ending up with copper toned tans.

John Mark and I spread our interests in a much broader spectrum including parks, zoos, street sights, and shady places away from the ever present sun. Like all good things, once their golden tans were in place the girls were ready for something new. "I think I'll call Homer Rugwell!!," I said. All three girls exclaimed "Dad, you must be kidding!" "But he's a missionary to Hawaii," I answered, "He lives just 20 miles up the island." "Dad, a missionary to Hawaii? What does he do? Hand out gospel tracts to the beach combers?" Even when Homer visited our state-side church to raise funds for his work on Oahu it was difficult to make the appeal sound credible. Ministry in Hawaii is not exactly in the same category as serving God behind the iron curtain. "Lets investigate," I offered, "What does a missionary do in Hawaii?"

The island seemed so heavenly that God didn't seem so necessary. I called Homer Rugwell who told me to check out of the hotel. We could all come and live with him. Late that same night, our luggage was again in a pile at our agreed meeting place. Homer was late. He had become a bit mixed up as to our agreed point of contact. Even the ocean beach seemed closed by the time Homer arrived. A little easy going but very kind, Homer was full of surprises. He did pastor a real church. We in fact attended service filled with real people. Missionary Rugwell had a true burden for the laid-back island dwellers. Our opinions changed and our time with Homer was really from God. We were taken in the Rugwell Volkswagon van to the nearby Polynesian Cultural Center – a tremendous place well worth seeing. We were given use of the V.W. to explore the island, from pineapple plantations to the rain forests and deserts of Oahu. I made one more phone call, this time to the island of Maui and to a name given by a friend before leaving for our trip. "This family will receive you," I was told. "In fact, I hope you will visit them." I did receive a most warm invitation to visit this "former preacher become millionaire" and his wife. We all agreed my three daughters would move back to Honolulu to the hotel and beach, and John Mark and I would go check out Maui.

The short island shuttle flight is really just up and back down. My Maui contact was for real. John Mark and I were met by a very stylish couple who led us directly to a beautiful Lincoln Continental Limousine and whisked us away wide eyed to their new home on a hill above the white sand beaches and calm blue Pacific. John Mark and I discreetly pinched each other to make sure we were not dreaming. We were not dreaming; for two days we were shown the sites. We saw the old Whaling Port of Lanai turned modern, and the world's largest banyan tree covering the largest part of a city lot. The final evening called for John Mark to be entertained at our host's home, and me to go out to dinner with them. I tried my luck at ordering Pacific Rim cuisine. I did poorly, not recognizing a single item on my plate either by taste or appearance. I thought I had at least ordered something familiar, especially with my host's very lovely wife helping me. Two things were explained to me after the meal. My plate contained squid, eel, jelly fish, shark meat, and some unknown substances. The second fact

I learned was that my order, so carefully worked out by my beautiful helper, was changed by her less helpful husband after it was sent in. I was congratulated for my bravery and informed that neither of my hosts had tried most of the things I had eaten. At the airport the next morning I was strongly encouraged to come back to visit anytime, and stay as long as I wished. I returned to Maui much sooner than any of us ever expected.

Back at Honolulu, Beth felt she was now needed at home. Our two weeks on the island had been full and satisfying. Lynn, Marliss and John Mark were willing to return home with Beth if I felt to stay on another week or two. A couple of days later I saw my children off on their return home and I flew back to Maui. I wanted absolute quiet time to just fast and pray and try to hear from God for my future. The whole situation turned out to be perfect. With a ground level room to myself, the beach less than a mile away, and perfect agreement with my hosts, I was set. I began a fast from food, and everything else but water that lasted nearly a week. The carefree and happy days with my children had been a great therapy to my spirit. These quiet days would bring healing to my soul. The beach was very nearly deserted on the first morning I arrived under the great trees near its edge. I parked the loaned vehicle, gathered up my Bible, water, towel and suntan lotion and headed toward a sheltered spot two hundred yards away. I was more than a little startled when two shapely, nude, female forms rose up from behind a sand dune a hundred feet from me. These absolutely golden tanned creatures didn't look around, and simply made their way to the water. Maybe they were mermaids, I just don't remember seeing any flippers. In the several days I returned to that extraordinary stretch of white sand only a very few other humans did I see.

Sea and sky and the gull's cry were really my only companions during that timeless span I spent on that lovely Maui beach. The spot I chose to remain – in the shade of several large well-leafed trees – had a very unusual feature. When I first viewed the site, I saw what appeared to be a gigantic coconut protruding up out of the white sand. A closer inspection revealed a cement bunker, a remainder from the World War II South Pacific conflict. This bunker proved to be a perfect back rest, and its domed top a place to lie up high enough to catch the cool sea breeze. My days were a study in total simplicity. No wonder hundreds of hippies overran this spot before they were expelled for various reasons. Returning to my hosts' house a little earlier in the afternoon than usual, I sat and visited for a couple of hours before going to my room for the night. The days by myself on the beach were just what I needed. I felt something good happening in my soul. The lady of the house responded to my request for some milk toast ending my fast. A most unusual experience occurred to me during that extraordinary night.

An unbroken sleep carried me past midnight until exactly 3:00 a.m. I was awakened by a clear voice speaking into my consciousness. "You shall have a special dispensation for a short duration," I was told. I had no time to see or question the speaker. The next instant I found myself at the edge of a most indescribable park-like garden. The sense of peace, comfort, light, and beauty was exhilarating. My eyes fell upon the figure of a person seated among cascading ropes of roses falling down over a magnificent stone wall. At that instant, a most beautiful woman looked my way, and upon seeing me sprang to her feet and ran toward me. In great surprise I recognized the angelic being as my wife Margie. We embraced in deep delight and continued to hold each other as we began talking. To this day that heavenly conversation has not come back to me. Not one word! I'm sure questions were answered somewhere in my deepest being. It was obvious Margie was extremely happy. A small understanding came quickly to me. Our love was still deep and real, but Margie didn't really belong to me anymore. She belonged in this realm that made earth's most dazzling beauty seem drab. Margie then looked away from me to her right. I followed her gaze and saw a carousel-appearing structure, all covered with flowers some distance away. People were coming out of the flowered doorways. Margie stepped back from me and said, "Oh, I must go, there is someone I must meet!" This woman, much more beautiful than I remembered her on earth, ran lightly over the green carpeted ground, stopped, turned fully toward me, and waved goodbye. I was instantly back in the darkness on Maui, sitting up in bed with my arms wrapped around my knees shaking quite strongly. It was as if my re-entry to this world was a shock to my system.

I slowly relaxed and stretched out in the predawn darkness. The clear voice I had heard earlier spoke again. "You must cast the shrouds of sorrow from you," I was told, "or it will take your strength." I laid quietly in a state of pleasant peace until the lovely Pacific dawn. A new day broke for me. I was healed in my soul and spirit. I left Maui a new man, ready to take up my life again. I thanked my wonderful hosts, flew back to Honolulu and on home to Idaho.

To successfully handle great loss and overcome deep sorrow is to escape in its truest sense. I had accomplished both. There was yet a major obstacle blocking my way into the great open room of discovery called reality. I was not yet free from a very significant mind set. Somehow the project that Margie and I had embarked upon must be completed. My dream church building, my promise to the town and people must be kept. No way could I, or would I, break my commitment to this monumental undertaking. Only a sovereign act of God could deter me or convince me otherwise. This act of God would take place because I was destined to escape into reality.

The remaining weeks of the summer passed quickly, and fall and school rushed my family into a settled routine. Lynn and Marliss placed our home onto a schedule. We were on our own for breakfast, none of us wanted much. I rose to great heights in preparing a scrambled egg on English muffin toast for John Mark and myself, after the girls departed for their schools. Supper was our time together. We would have a very nice meal prepared by Lynn and Marliss in the excellent style Margie had taught them. Beth and Glen, now living in nearby Spokane, added their visits, support, and comfort to our household.

Money began coming in for the building of People's Church. Materials were donated including a huge stack of 24-inch floor beams, enough to begin the proposed multi-purpose building. The date was set to begin construction on the first unit of a planned million-dollar project. When winter snow melted and the frost would leave the ground, the basement for the first unit would be dug. Excitement began building on a special Sunday morning as the northbound sun began to warm North Idaho's earth. The congregation of People's Church all gathered at the property. Ten acres were dedicated for the new church, and earth was symbolically opened for the first building. The planning and activities were good for me. Between duties at home, school, and church, I was kept very busy.

      A year had skipped by since the solemn grave-side farewell to Margie. It was time to move ahead full speed, capturing excitement and momentum to attract the city and its people. The night before the equipment was to excavate the first basement, I came home from the mid-high school feeling less than well. I begged out of a shopping trip with a friend, and went to bed. Because of my illness, John Mark went to his own bed that night. The girls saw to my comforts before saying goodnight. During the night my condition worsened. I called Lynn early the next morning and had her call the mid-high asking them to obtain a substitute for me. I told the children to go on to school, I would be fine. My diagnosis for my ailment was the flu, the Hong Kong and London variety put together. During that morning cramps and great pain settled in my abdominal area. I called the part-time church secretary and told her to ask the church prayer group to pray for me. "Oh, by the way, call Dr. Cederbloom and tell him I have the flu. Get me some Pepto-Bismol and Milk of Magnesia." Evelyn was prompt, a few minutes later she arrived with my self-prescribed remedy. She gave me the doctor's prescription for the flu and the Pepto-Bismol and Milk of Magnesia I had ordered. I took the flu pills, a generous portion of Milk of Magnesia, and topped everything off with the Pepto-Bismol for good measure. My cramps increased, the flu pills seemed to explode in my empty stomach. The Pepto-Bismol seemed to get lost in all of this. I began to perspire; something had to be done. I was losing strength, my head was aching, the pain was increasing, the cramps were becoming unbearable. I found an enema bag, dragged myself to the bathroom and proceeded to give myself a warm soap suds water enema. My exhausting effort brought me no relief. I felt weaker as if I might pass out. Getting back to my bed was not easy to do. I forced myself to phone my secretary the second time and fortunately found her at her home. "Evelyn," I gasped, "call Dr. Cederbloom, tell him the flu medicine isn't helping me." Collapsing on the bed I passed into a semi-conscious state.

The next thing I remember, Evelyn was shaking me and ordering me to get up. "You must go the hospital. Dr. Cederbloom will meet us there." Another woman who also came with Evelyn helped half carry and drag me up the split level stairway to the front door on into an idling vehicle. Much of my being admitted, prepped and ready for surgery was a blur of hasty action. Dr. Cederbloom did say to me, as I lay in a large vat of ice cubes to lower the 106 degree temperature that was raging in my body, "Reverend Clarke, when we see someone in great pain bent over holding their side, we do tend to suspect appendicitis rather than the Hong Kong flu." Being the gentleman I was I didn't ask the good doctor why he prescribed the flu medication sight unseen. Actually I didn't care at that point. "I do need to tell you Reverend Clarke," the Doctor added, "we are very concerned about you. Your appendix probably has been ruptured for about eighteen hours. It's likely that peritonitis has set in. We'll do the best we can. Doctor Thompson will perform the surgery, I'll scrub and be there." In the waiting area outside of surgery, I began the brief count down to deep unconsciousness.

After surgery I was taken to intensive care. The vigil was to see if I would live or die. How long I lay in the deep darkness between life and death, I'm not quite sure. The first awareness that came to me while still in an unconscious state was light beginning to fill the intensive care room where I was laying. The light grew from bright to brilliant. From the corner of the hospital room, the brilliant light moved toward my bed. A form and face so bright they were most difficult to make out distinctly stopped by my bedside and spoke to me. "I have taken your life from you, now I'm giving it back to you. Should you so choose, you can build the church you have planned. I will bless you and many will come even by the hundreds." The personage of warmth and peace continued to speak. "If you will trust me, I will lead you by a way you have never gone before. I will give you a message you have never ministered, to a people you have never known." Sometime after this most unusual divine visitation, I began to slowly float upward out of the deep state of unconsciousness I had been in for many hours.

Coming back to consciousness was in slow motion with soft shades of light and sounds. As my eyes slowly opened, I stared blankly at what appeared to be a mountain of fuzzy snowballs near the head of my bed. Seeking something familiar, my gaze moved on to other areas nearby. Containers, tubes and apparatuses around the space above my head were of no help. A quiet voice, spoken from somewhere to my left, brought me to a rapid state of awareness. "Well Reverend, you had yourself quite a sleep!" A nurse dressed in white standing nearby helped bring everything into focus. "How long have I been out?" I croaked, not recognizing my voice. "Too long!" responded the special nurse. "Your children are very anxious. I must let them see you immediately." Just as the white-clad nurse turned to summon my children, I asked her about the huge basket of gauze bandages by my bed. "Oh, those? Well, frankly, the doctor expected the bandages to float off of your incision." Before I would ask any more she was gone. "Dad!" my girls all cried out in unison, "You really had us frightened! The doctors were not giving you a very big chance to survive!" John Mark wanted to see my stitches which were not yet on display. "Girls," I told my three daughters, "I think I've just been given a second chance! I'll have to tell you all what happened sometime. One thing I know, I'm going to be okay." It was true. No peritonitis, no serious complications. It did take time to get out of the hospital. This had nothing to do with my surgery. Anemia and a staph infection held up a rapid recovery. From this point on everything seemed to fall into step with a grand design far beyond my comprehension. It was as if a predetermined plan was brought into operation for my life. My full escape into reality was only months away.

When change is in the air, danger is always in the wind. The lesser choice always presents itself just before the perfect one. He who keeps his options open while searching for the very best is wise.

Psalms 55:8

I would hasten my escape from the windy storm and tempest.

CHAPTER THIRTEEN

COUNTDOWN

Flowers and visitors filled my room over the next few days, all with the same hint of expectancy. "Up and out, pastor, you have things to do!" No question about it, there was much that awaited me. My ultimate dream – the church building and growth project, the ten acres hidden in timber on a hill above Coeur d'Alene Lake, and even plans for a new home – were before me.

Another dream came to me though during my recuperation that created a great dilemma. From this point on, all my plans died in my breast. In this dream I found myself standing outside a small town similar to the town where I now lived. It appeared that people were leaving their homes and going somewhere. Doors stood open and I could see empty rooms inside. Each of the departing people took only one thing with them, a small satchel on their side held by a strap over their shoulders. I was conveyed from one village or city to another. The same scene was repeated. Out of the general population, some people left their homes and belongings behind. Greatly puzzled in the dream after seeing all of this, I stood on the street in the last town and questioned what this was all about. Although nothing of danger could be seen yet, I concluded the only reason people would leave like that was there had to be either flood, fire or war. While I was still assimilating all this, I felt a weight on my shoulder. Looking down, I saw a strap and satchel hanging on my side, exactly like those people I saw leaving.

The strange effect this dream had on me was to kill completely any desire for any of the plans that had been the driving force of my life up to that moment. To make problems worse, there was absolutely no one with whom I could share any of this unexplainable experience.

One of the visitors to my hospital room was Dan Hunt. Dan, full of energetic excitement, was a mover. Dan spun a chair around and straddled it with its back facing me. "Pastor, you've got to get back to church," was Dan's opening line. Before I could answer with, "Tell me something else new," he continued. "There's a new lady who just started coming, she's a knockout! I don't think she has a husband." "Dan!" I protested, "A woman is the last thing I'm interested in right now!" "You just wait," my blond bundle of energy proclaimed. "I've got a ball game, see you later, but don't forget, you've got to see this new lady." With that, Dan was gone like a pleasant breeze that blew in and out of my room.

To attend church was out of the question for the next day, but I did manage to do so a week later, just barely. The strep condition still persisted and my incision, though healing okay, was draining a bit. "Doctor," I begged when the surgeon showed up the next time to see me, "I really do need to make an appearance at church soon. You see," I explained half jokingly, "my contract requires me to show up with Bible in hand once a month." It had been actually over a month since I had been at the church. "Okay Reverend, I'd hate to see you lose your job. You can go Sunday on this condition – I want you back in the hospital within three hours." Wow, just like the first liberty when I was in the Navy! "Thanks Doctor," I said to his retreating back, as Doctor Thompson went out the door.

I did arrive at the 11 o'clock service at People's Church the next Sunday. My three daughters arrived an hour before church time at my room with suit, tie, and white shirt. I didn't quite appear my dapper self in my Sunday finery. My back was slightly corkscrewed from the effect of the staff infection, and I bent a bit at the waist from the pull of my incision. The brief appearance I made at church was far from impressive. Limping to the pulpit and making a very short greeting was all I could muster. For anyone seeing me for the first time, I'm sure they must have wondered, "Is that the leader?" The new lady Dan Hunt had mentioned was in the service. In fact, she made a prayer request, a common practice in our meetings. "Please pray," she asked in a musical voice, "I need a job and a house to rent." My first thought was not too benevolent. Her two major needs will take some good-sized prayers. Dan was right, was my second thought. This lady is very nice looking, you can bet there is a husband not far away. The girls whisked me off immediately after the dismissal for dinner at home before returning me to my cell at the Kotami Memorial Hospital.

Within a couple more weeks I went back to my duties at the People's Church. However, I never really fully returned. I went through the motions, but my heart just wasn't in it. Try as I may, I could not conjure up the former excitement I had held for everything involved. The whole thing for some unexplainable reason was dead within me. I'm sure my close call with death, because of the ruptured appendix had something to do with my new outlook. The reality of how weak our true grip is on the thing called existence, definitely affected me.

It is said that everyone who has a life and death crisis is never the same again. All individuals who have such an experience will either draw nearer to God or seem to pull away from Him. No one has given a good reason for the later case. Possibly since death is an ultimate experience, it can only have one or the other effect on a person. In my case, which for me was of Grace, I seemed more given to deeper spiritual things. A new desire for greater divine reality came to me. I seemed to know there was more to be obtained in spiritual experience and knowledge. Revelation and searching the scripture stood like an open door which I had never noticed or sought before. Now, a God-given hunger made itself known in my awareness. Losing my precious wife Margie, then my standing in the denomination I had loved and given myself to totally for more than twenty years, was like having rare treasures torn from my grasp. Facing the possible loss of my own life broke eggshell-thin encasement around me. I was literally birthed into a new reality. I could truly see that life is very fragile at best. Dearest treasures can slip like sand through our fingers. Hard earned reputation can easily be peeled off like old wall paper. Ambition can turn stale and sour like an undigested meal in ones stomach. Fulfillment has a way of vanishing like the rainbow after a brief summer shower. Just hearing the beat of a new drummer can cause old and long time loyalties to fracture and fade. For me, the high tide of God's dealing had come in and swept clean the beaches of my life. I stood quiet and waiting in the aftermath of my spiritual cleansing, not at all sure of what had happened or was yet going to happen to me. God did not remind me of the proposal he made to me in the hospital intensive care unit. I did not ponder how all of that might work out should I consider taking him up on the deal. Everything lay just as it was left that dark night of my crisis. That decision would not be a matter of, "Yes I will," then, "Please sign here." Looking back, what would happen was a series of events each requiring a decision. The decisions would chart the course of action. Action would be the way I would answer God's proposition. At this most critical juncture in my life, a major divine intervention occurred.

One year and a half had passed since I was parted from Margie. Needless to say, I greatly missed the companionship I had enjoyed for so many happy years with Margie. My daughters and son filled in a very real way, along with the church, the lonely corner of my life. I was, however, counseled by a pastor friend to consider some casual female friendship. I must admit, I had noticed an increase in our church attendance of unattached, hungry-looking women.

My first awareness of the potential dangers in this area came when I agreed to a suggestion made by Bud Actipus, my self-appointed lonely heart counselor. He told me of a single's group meeting at a Spokane city suburban residence. "Nice Christian folks," he said. "Bring a steak and come on over," the contact I was given told me by phone. "We'll have a steak fry and fellowship." Very low key and casual, I decided after I arrived and stored my uncooked steak in a refrigerator. Near the kitchen, I could hear sports casting from the Olympic games then in progress. Settling in a cozy corner with a good view of the giant screen, I was gone. Everything else faded away for nearly two and a half hours. I simply orbited into oblivion, forgetting where I was, or for what purpose I had come. I came to when a strange woman bent down in front of me wanting to know if I had cooked my steak. Mumbling something about not knowing how, I was led away to be taught. The affair was breaking up, and I'd really not gotten acquainted with anyone. Many had found companions and were leaving together. I ended up left with four women who needed rides home. When I took one look at these lonely, hungry-looking creatures, the jeopardy of my situation dawned on me. Anyway, I would try to manage. I would end up alone with one of the women in my car. Choosing to let each one off like a bus route working my way toward Couer d'Alene, I ended up with a widowed school teacher. "Please come in," she begged, "You don't have to drive home tonight!" My first thought was, "How do I get out of this?" My next thought was of what I planned to do to my counsel, Bud Actipis, who had gotten me into all this. I committed a much lesser sin by lying about critically ill children, and extremely early appointments, then fled.

Bud Actipis struck once more. He called to tell me he had invited a very eligible and lovely widow to my church. "Just check her out is all I ask," he told me. "She is a former Idaho Senator's wife." Sure enough, the deceased senator's wife's name was sent to the pulpit one Sunday morning among the visitor's cards. At the door after church, I determined to be warm, polite, and discrete. I had to admit that the woman I judged to be the widow, was most attractive, actually a raven-haired beauty. I may have been a slight bit long on warmth, and maybe a little short on discretion. I bent over a lengthy hand shake calling her by name, murmuring how happy I was to meet her. "Oh, I'm not who you think I am," I was told. "My friend here is the one whose name you said." From behind the center of my attendant stepped a lady I hadn't even seen until then! She was short, shy, and of a more blond appearance than her dark-haired friend. I uttered an inane, quiet apology while the two ladies slipped past me and out the church doors. Neither of these two ever appeared in the church again while I was pastor. I didn't have to wonder why! Two sputtering brushes with what counselor "Bud" called female friendship served to prove I was on very uncertain ground.

Meeting an unmarried classmate, Rae, at a high school class reunion, and agreeing to travel to Seattle for a second reunion with her never happened. The weekend was planned, the schedule cleared, even my green Buick Lesabre serviced and topped off with fuel. I had my daughter, Lynn, drop me off at the Centex Station, and I waved her on since I was all set. The shining Buick waiting in a parking space ready to go. Slipping behind the wheel, I turned the key in the ignition, and was stunned by the loud clatter coming from the engine. In shock, I shut down the noisy machine, got out, and went in to see the manager. "Hey Art, come out and listen to my Buick. Something has happened to it." Big, handsome, Art Grant, with his perpetual smile in place said, "Let's go and take a listen." The sounds like an old threshing machine coming from under the four door sedan hood removed the smile from manager Art's face. "I need to talk to my new service man, Mr. Grant," he muttered more to himself than to me. The engine was threshed ruin! I would be going nowhere that weekend. Any spark from a few times out with another woman from the church, younger than me, blinked out when she decided to go see friends she had known prior to her conversion in the Nevada Lake Idaho area. Then came Nathel, the new lady at church who possessed the musical voice.

Reality is the present Divine Truth applied experientially today. It is living daily in a state of true spiritual understanding and ballance. Reality is our current healthy relationship with the Lord Jesus Christ, revealing the now of our spiritual condition, the strength of our inner person. Reality is existing moment by moment in the life flow of God.

2 Corinthians 8:11 (KJV)

Now therefore perform the doing of it; that as there was a readiness to will, so there may be a performance also out of that which ye have.

CHAPTER FOURTEEN

REALITY

My first conversation with Nathel was in regard to a profound sermon I preached called, "A Church Without Walls." I proclaimed that the church should be open to all, regardless of station or status in life. Yes, a church for all the people! Nathel first informed me that she found my "word", as she called it, interesting. But why, she wanted to know, if you have a vision for a church without walls, are you planning to build such a huge church building? Nathel's next question, in common vernacular, blew me away. "What if the Lord told you to hold your services over by the lake sometime like He did?" I thought to myself, "That's not what I mean by a church without walls. Of course, you always build a building! The bigger the better." I noticed an older lady standing next to Nathel watching all this with an amused smile on her face. "Well Sister, you've given me something to think about," I responded, and turned back to shake hands with a few stragglers also leaving the church. Nathel and her friend, whose name turned out to be Elsie, made their way with a couple of children to an old beater of a Ford sedan at the outer edge of the parking lot. Up close I found Nathel to be very pretty. She seemed relaxed, yet in control. There was something serene about her bearing. Services by the lake sometime?! What about seating and bathrooms, and how would you take the offering?

I made my way to "stinky", the non-affectionate name my family had given to our second car, a stubborn, small, black English Ford. No progress had been made on my Buick engine repair. I would have to rent or borrow another vehicle. The same Sunday night I made a small appeal for the use of anyone's second auto. I explained that our second vehicle was needed for my children's school transportation. Concluding by saying, "Just think about my request and let me know." I then waited. My vision was for some hot little sports car to race about fulfilling my pastoral duties. No sports car was offered me. At our next general church meeting, I again made my request. No offers came forth. "Hey, It wasn't my fault the engine in my Buick blew," I explained. "The service man forgot to put oil in after he drained the old out." At that moment, from the middle of the congregation, the new lady raised her hand. "Elsie and I each have a car, you can use one of ours." Remembering Nathel's battered older bomber, I thought this wasn't exactly what I had hoped for. "Thank you, Sister," I quietly answered and went on to other announcements.

After the meeting, Nathel met me at the church door. "When do you want to take our car?" she asked me brightly as if she and Elsie were offering me the use of a new BMW. I had been praying that a last-minute offer would be made by some hold out on my way from the pulpit to the back door. No offers had come. I was faced with accepting or refusing Elsie and Nathel's tired old 4-wheel pony. "Let's go look," I stalled. The closer we came to the offered vehicle, the more my apprehension grew. Several dings showed up in the lights of the parking lot. My eyes then spotted the tires. They were absolutely bald, slicker than a banana peeling. Nathel saw me view the tires and confidently announced, "We came all the way from California, not one flat." Before I had a chance to refuse, Nathel handed me the keys to the brave old vehicle and said, "If you will take us to our house, you can take the Ford home with you tonight." I was stuck. The battered old Ford with its four slick tires would be my transportation for the foreseeable future.

By now both of Nathel's earlier prayer requests had been answered. She had landed a job and found a house to rent at her price and liking. Dan Hunt, who had first told me about the new lady at church, steered Nathel to an opening at the bank where I had my account. The house was the doings of Ruth, the teacher of the Sunday School class Nathel and Elsie attended. John Mark, who had followed me out to inspect the loaner auto, was now giving the two children I had seen earlier, information, I'm sure, concerning the local scene. I waved my daughters on, and they and Stinky moved away leaving a cloud of black exhaust smoke. I was asked to drive, and was surprised that the Ford started up okay, and the engine didn't make any ominous noises. As I let everyone out at their rental on Ninth Street, Elsie said, "Oh Pastor Clarke, please

148

pray that my car will sell. I don't think I'll need it since I'm living with Nathel and her children." I promised to do so, sure that there would be no quick action since Elsie's vehicle didn't look any better than the one I had borrowed. Elsie said one more thing as John Mark and I prepared to drive away, "Please come and visit us soon, when you have time." I visited the house on Ninth Street much sooner than I ever intended.

Three days after I took Nathel's car home to use, she gave me some very alarming news at the Wednesday night prayer and Bible study meeting. "Pastor Clarke, you must have really prayed," Nathel and Elsie told me, "Elsie's car sold! The first man who came to look paid cash! Its wonderful, but now we have a problem," Nathel went on. "Now I don't have a way to get to my job at the bank." My head was doing a small spin. The lovely damsel was in distress. What was a gentleman to do? My Buick should have been repaired long ago. No one expected Elsie"s auto to sell so quickly. Now I was driving Nathel's Ford, and she had no way to get to her work. The choice was simple to see. Either I give back the borrowed car to Nathel or see that she had a ride to and from the bank. At this moment Martin, Nathel's quiet 11 or 12 year old son, spoke up. "Why doesn't Pastor just drive Mom to work? Then he can still use the car the rest of the time."

So it was, I began driving Nathel to and from her work at the bank. What was only going to be a few days duty stretched out to over a month. It seemed that my Buick was stuck in quick sand, the needed GMC parts lost in the bottom of the ocean, and the workers encased in axle grease at forty below zero. That Nathel and I got acquainted did not have the most favorable ratio of chance as might appear on the surface. She and Elsie had moved to Couer d'Alene believing they were guided by God to do so. Both had come from a small, obscure, peripheral fellowship of born again Spirit-filled believers. This group, and others like them, mostly held home worship services. Nathel and Elsie were not looking for a Pentecostal-type church like ours or a semi-swinging preacher like me. I also soon learned that Nathel was not looking for a man.

Alone for nearly ten years, after a brief and fragile marriage had shattered, Nathel had raised her children by herself, singing her way through the hard places. Deserted by her husband after two small children and a tiny infant, Nathel was left to paddle her own canoe. Her husband was then fully free to pursue drinking, gambling, and women, which for some time prior he had put above his marriage. Nathel and her little crew were much like survivors from a ship that sank, making their way to land on their own, no longer looking for rescue ships. Why did Nathel loan me her car? With her and Elsie it was a way of life. Anyone could have borrowed their car. I'm sure someone from off the street would have been considered also.

Seeing each other morning and night helped Nathel and me get acquainted much more rapidly than would otherwise have ever been possible. My first shock upon entering the house on Ninth Street, surrounded by giant shade trees and vast parking lot, was the absence of furniture. A couch, kitchen table, and a few chairs was all I could see on the main floor. Nathel gave no explanation or made any embarrassing apology. It was soon obvious her wardrobe was of simple tastes, and even a little limited in my opinion. This beautiful lady stepped out of her front door that first morning I came by to take her to work as relaxed and confident as if she were dressed in the latest styles. I did drive the old Ford into the tire shop and had four new tires put on. My faith certainly didn't come near Nathel's. I would not have driven out of town on the paper thin skins she had trusted all the way from California.

It didn't take me long to summarize Nathel's life style. One word said it all, simplicity. Her whole approach to life was based on a child-like faith in God. Mr. Leon Doane, Nathel's boss, himself a Christian, called me into his office on my next visit to the bank. "What do you think of my new personal secretary?" he asked me. "She's a Christian!" "Yes, I know," I confessed. "How's she doing?" "Great," Leon told me. "She has never worked in a bank before. She has a lot to learn, but she'll do just fine. What Nathel lacks in knowledge she makes up in faith," he added.

Spring and summer slid by. Nathel's parents came from California bringing a small trailer-load of household things. Next came the elders from the small Roseville California fellowship. They were on the scene to check out the preacher and the church Nathel, Elsie and children were attending. I was not given a five star rating, I later learned. I was judged by the elders to be too agreeable and smooth to suit them.

The big progress in any relationship with Nathel and her family came via my son John Mark. He and Martin and sister Ann, hit it off great. Unknown to me, John Mark had tried to cut a deal with Nathel to go into a business venture with him. He envisioned a peewee golf course, using Nathel's Ninth Avenue large front yard. John Mark told Nathel he could get plenty of golf balls from his dad's golf bag. I did invite Nathel and Elsie to lunch at a restaurant near the bank one day for a specific reason. I wanted to find out just where they were really coming from spiritually. It was clear from little indications that these two woman had a different spiritual orientation from that of our church. All kinds of people had come down the pike over the years with all kinds of ideas, especially in the Pentecostal realm. I think I had seen and heard of nearly everything – from the far out religious nuts claiming to be Elijah, to a variety of tent healers, real and bizarre. I still had a cry within me for reality, simplicity, and purity. There seemed to be an element of these qualities in Nathel and Elsie. With our orders in for lunch, I began to question these two relaxed and composed ladies.

"What is it with these home meetings and not having a church?" I wanted to know. "There are a couple things we could tell you," Nathel began. "The church is not a building, its the people. We are not going to the church to a meeting, we are the 'church' going somewhere to meet. Secondly, if the hundreds of millions, even billions, spent on extravagant church building programs was spent on missions, I imagine that the world could have been evangelized by now." Our food arrived, and I could see I'd have to speed up my questioning or go away from this lunch only slightly more informed than when we started. "Those songs you sing, they are different, especially the one about the Camel Train. I think I understand the one about wanting to walk in union with the Lord, but tell me about the Camel Train. How do the words go?"

"You know the story about Isaac and Rebekah, don't you, Pastor?" Elsie wanted to know. "The Holy Spirit is seeking a bride for Christ today, just like Eleazzar found Rebecca for Isaac in that day." To me that was Old Testament, for Jews; I was a New Testament preacher. "Have you heard of types and shadows?" I was asked. We had an older fellow come through one time with a dusty table-top model of the tabernacle of Moses, but his types and shadows didn't quite reach me and left me cold. The next and last question I announced as lunch time was slipping rapidly away, "Ruth Gish, our adult teacher, told me you both feel there is a reason why the church of today isn't reaching perfection. Could you tell me how you see all this?" Nathel declined desert and answered as if it was perfectly easy to see. "It takes the five-fold ministry to bring the church to perfection and the fullness of Christ," she stated. "Most churches have a one-man ministry, that of a pastor. The prophet and apostolic ministries, which are the foundation of the New Testament church have been left out." It was time to go. On our way to the faithful Ford, I shot one last question out into the air. "Are there any more people who believe like you?" Both Elsie and Nathel answered together, "Oh, yes, many, all over. Hundreds gather at a number of conventions every year where line upon line revelation is preached by a five-fold ministry." Leaving Nathel at the bank and Elsie at the big house on Ninth Street, I drove slowly home to do some thinking.

I did do some thinking – much more than my talk with Nathel and Elsie should have generated. It was as if a flood gate opened somewhere in my mind, and released years of accumulated thoughts. Bible prophecy and end-of-the-world kind of preaching was familiar to me. I had even done some of my own end-of-the-world preaching. On that particular day my train of thought ran a gamut of very serious reflections. Where was the world heading? Was time running out? What would decent people do or where could they go in a decaying society?

A film I had once seen came to mind, putting many things into perspective. In the movie called "The <u>Poseidon</u> Adventure," a luxury liner capsized in a strange storm at sea. This last voyage of the veteran of many an ocean crossings was exactly as it was supposed to be. Bought by an entrepreneur for scrap, the ship was being sailed to a dry dock on the East Coast of the U.S. from a port on the interior of the Gulf of

Mexico. The season was Christmas time, and a high festive spirit could be felt on each deck of the splendid old ship. One reason for the good spirits among the passengers was the extraordinary price for this magic cruise. The eight day journey was going to cost the lucky ticket holders only a few cents on the dollar of what should be the price. The very cheap fares would, however, be more than enough to cover the cost of moving the ship to dry dock. Everyone was very happy. Food and drinks were, of course, amply available. At the instance of the unusual sea tragedy, a gala party was in progress in the grand, ornate ball room. By now, the Poseidon had cleared the gulf and was some 30 - 40 miles off shore of the lower eastern U.S. cruising northward.

The first hint by those on the bridge that danger was upon them was the sight of a high solid wall of advancing sea water, coming toward the starboard of the doomed ship at 60 miles per hour. No warning could be given, the ship was simply bowled over and left floating upside down in the aftermath of the freak earthquake which caused tidal waves. The real story now begins.

What happened to those who didn't die in the first lethal blow to the proud aged ship? The one thing most of those still alive could not adjust to was that the crippled ship was upside down, totally at the mercy of the sea. Only six to eight feet of the bottom of the fan tail section of the ship could be seen by flying sea gulls when the sea returned to its former relative calmness.

Few people respond calmly to extreme crisis. Heroes are made at such times, but most make mistakes which cost them their lives. Lights were basically out. A few emergency bulbs burned dimly in this upside down world. Everything was the reverse of natural orientation. Passengers would crawl out of the companion ways, force open doors only to fall downward toward the ceiling of the ball room. Death or serious injury followed. Any hope of escape from the slowly flooding, topsy-turvy steel casket went against every instinct of common reason. The trapped inmates of this watery prison would have to make their way upward toward the bottom of the ship, to the engine room propeller area. Next, only a prayer for outside help to open an escape hole through the steel hull could save them.

The plight of the survivors of the Poseidon is exactly the same as any of us born on extremely endangered Planet Earth. Our world is topsy-turvy. Systems on terra firma, in the political, economical, and ecology areas are breaking down. None are failsafe. The best minds are coming up with no answers. Nathel and Elsie did not awaken me to all this, God did. These two spiritual sisters were like gentle voices echoing some deeper stronger voice. Some brave souls did escape from death on the ship Poseidon. Help did come. A hole was cut through the one-inch steel plate, and survivors were lifted out to safety. Actually, their escape from the doomed Poseidon was a miracle. So may the escape of a small remnant of those of our times, who learn to swim against the tide, be a profound miracle. Our escape will be contrary to the reasoning of the natural mind.

The chief lesson of history is that no one has learned from the lessons of history. The classic mistakes made through time are only being compounded in our days. Millions are now affected overnight by one man's greed and murderous intent. Governmental economic blunders deepen the pit of recession and poverty in country after country. The age old practice of raising taxes by irresponsible politicians fails to bring an economic fix. A greater oppressive burden is placed on multitudes not able to survive the blow. It's almost like some gigantic plan in madness is succeeding.

The reality of our situation is that one must go against the grain, the trends, and the sweep of history. Multitudes of Christians expect a quick, safe, painless exit from the dilemma of our times. There simply will be no such escape. The miraculous exodus concept destroys the very element needed to survive – a proper mind set, and a survivor mode – which alone can provide the inner strength to endure the rip tide of the end of an age.

Mind set, preparation, and a plan has always been the hallmark of survivors. Ours is not merely an escape from a generation hell bent on their own destruction, morally, spiritually and physically. We must come out of the indescribable deception of it to come into reality.

The deception is simple. Man cannot by his own ability and reason work his way out of his disastrous dilemma. Reality – only God can bring the needed deliverance. The deception says things will turn around, they always have. Reality – things will only get worse, and that rapidly! Rather than having more time, the great count down has begun. Reality – no government and no man can pull the world out of its fatal tail spin. Mankind will continue on its irreversible course. I came to a strong positive conclusion during the two hours I was alone before my children came home from school. God alone had the answers, for me, my family, or the church and the world.

Nathel did play a part in my escape into reality. Our time together produced a friendship, and as weeks stretched into months, I found myself in love with this beautiful, uncomplicated woman who was "every inch" a lady. Stopping by Nathel's desk at the bank in late summer, I asked if her simple schedule ever allowed time to go out to dinner? She looked at me for a long moment before answering. With a slightly wistful look in her eyes, Nathel answered me. "It's been so long since I have gone out to dinner, I can't remember when." Then she brightened and said, "Yes, Mr. Clarke, I would love to go out to dinner with you." On the lovely drive from Couer d'Alene to Spokane, where we had dinner at a restaurant on the South Hill, Nathel taught me a song :

"Victory Oh Victory it is Mine, if I hold my peace, let the Lord fight my battles, Victory oh Victory it is mine!"

I would need and use the strength of that little tune many times in the years to come.

That evening was lovely, the meal splendid, and a tender bond was formed between Nathel and me that night. A few weeks later I proposed. Nathel didn't immediately accept. I was mildly surprised when she explained. "I could never promise to do anything this serious without asking counsel and confirmation from some 'ministries' I flow with and trust." In some strange way I seemed to understand.

I still asked a couple of questions. "How does this 'being sure' work?" was my first question. "How long will it take?" "I'll make a call," Nathel promised, "I'll know something tonight." To Nathel's surprise, someone named Frank and another named Sam said they had no "check". They promised to ask the "prophets" for confirmation. I think Nathel expected her friends to say, "Stay far away from this Pentecostal preacher!!" Confirmation came in a few days and was deemed to be positive. Only the timing seemed to be important. I was not given at the time too much to interpreting of visions by prophets. I told Nathel if timing was an important factor, then it must mean we should marry as soon as possible. We did marry soon. On November 12th, the day after my daughters, Marilyn and Marliss, had their birthdays we were married in a private family-only wedding. Nathel stood sober and beautiful by the stairs in the front room of the large house on Ninth Street. There was quiet peace on that wedding day, and two families of children were bonded together.

A profound miracle followed. From what my church secretary, Evelyn, called the ingredients of an atomic bomb, and Nathel's bank boss, Leon, called a fluke, God brought deep affection in the children for each other – not all at once, but slowly and surely. Within months many who did not know us well would ask which children belonged to Nathel or to me. Our answer was always the same. "They all belong to both of us!" Even when someone would persist and try to guess they were usually wrong. From that wedding day, my life changed dramatically. Purpose, goals, direction and incentives simply took new form. The dreams of a large church overflowing with people lay dead in my breast. No longer did I secretly think of the prospects or possibility of high district or even national office in my denomination. I was already once removed from such a possibility. The direction of my life took a major turn. Never again would I be involved as a one man pastor of the local church. Within a few short years, I would be catapulted into a world-wide ministry that would carry me like a marathoner from nation to nation.

Most important came a mantle of simplicity over my life. Plans for a honeymoon to Hawaii were dropped as they paled, no longer relevant to the life that lay before Nathel and me. Renting a small trailer, we learned of a few hundred people who were gathering for a convention near Palm Springs, California. We climbed into the high country south of Palm Springs, and arrived at an abandoned Boy Scout camp rented by this unnamed group of which Nathel had some small contact and knowledge. A late November storm piled ten inches of snow on the ground, and greeted us the next morning as we left our snug little trailer to attend the meeting scheduled for after breakfast. What I began to hear that day and for several services afterward was quickened to my spirit. It was as if I had been born to hear such a message. I was hearing many things stated clearly for the first time, yet deep within me something said, "I've always known that!" What I began to hear was much more than the letter of the Word or the truth behind the letter. There was a new vibrant life behind the letter and truth. The "more" that I had always known existed somewhere began to be spoken of in that very simple, even stark setting on that small California mountaintop. A brand of practical, lived-out holiness and purity was spoken of that was within reach of every believer. Death to selfishness, and the ability to live a laid-down life, before only attributed to a few historic saints and martyrs, was now being practiced. God's will on earth, thus His kingdom come, was an immediate hope pounding now in the breasts of men and women. The final spiritual Feast of Tabernacles was preached as the present truth. A quality of love, transcending natural affection, and mutually benefiting relationships began to reveal a top rung call. Koinenia! This was a level of divine love shed abroad in hearts, and able to bring pure relationships not tainted with natural earthly drawings. Yet marriage remained a pattern of Christ's love for His church and young people were encouraged to begin restoring a wholesome example of love, courtship, and marriage. Keeping themselves pure, while establishing a spiritual bond that would endure forever, regardless of whether a positive confirmation followed a period of time of waiting on the Spirit for a true witness. These young people would live in respect for each other, offering the other unto the Lord.

Much more would follow and a Spirit of revelation fell on me during those days that opened up God's marvelous Book as never before. Back in Couer d'Alene I sold my split level home, sold off the vast surplus of nearly everything I had collected, and our combined family moved into the big, shaded house on Ninth Street. The church I had founded, knowing that I no longer carried the vision for their future, agreed quickly to my resignation. A lovely post-wedding dinner and gifts were given to Nathel and me. Suddenly we stood like a traveler at the crest of a high place, looking out into a future, across valleys and distant mountain ranges. I had absolutely no sense of loss. I stood on that high place that day knowing that much more lay out there ahead of me than I had left behind. Like a soaring eagle riding a strong draft, I felt freedom under my wings. My escape was not from a denomination or the church I had birthed. My escape was from some deep snare within. A prison door opened in my inner being letting me out of the cell holding me in the power of wrong motives, doing seemingly right things for the wrong reasons. I could say with David in the Psalms, "The snare is broken and I am escaped." The earthly tug on my soul was broken. Things, style, place, and position loosened their hold on me. Like David, I could say, "My soul escapes like a bird." I was free.

... at last unencumbered from all the earthly realm in order to take hold of all in the heavenly...

John 8:32

You shall know the truth, and the truth shall make you free.

John 8:36

If the Son therefore shall make you free, you shall be free indeed.

Romans 8:2

The law of the spirit of life in Christ Jesus hath made me free from the law of sin and death.

CHAPTER FIFTEEN

FREEDOM

The man or woman who cannot be bought or sold, who can have nothing taken from them or added to them, who can stand at last in that rare place where they have nothing to gain or lose – at that point they are able to stay or go, hold fast, or let loose. Then, that man and that woman have tasted what freedom is all about.

Freedom is the total lack of "self" consciousness. A place in which the fires of selfishness lie dead and cold, as ashes in ones heart. Expectation and idealism lie buried in some unmarked silent crypt. Only a growing awareness remains, a knowing that absolute joy will be found in becoming servant of all, finding out that giving fully, and freely, is the ultimate virtue. Learning that it is possible to live in a state of great tolerance for everyone and everything, forgiveness becomes a way of life, and memory functions void of offense. Freedom is a state where love never fails.

Should all this seem beyond the grasp of or experience of one who may read these words, a simple fact must be remembered. With man such things are impossible, but with God all things are possible. When a man or woman leaps free from the captivity of their own mentality, liberty comes in that instant. Natural reason, no matter how articulate or pulsating with pure genius, is the tomb of the mind. Someone wisely stated that all knowledge is, at best, vanity. Imagine your spirit imprisoned inside your body, depending only on the natural senses to gain any understanding of life and death. Just think, if you had only your sense of touch, taste, hearing, seeing and smell to learn of heaven and hell, time and eternity?

Captivity is having no spiritual contact with the wisdom and knowledge of the universe found in God. Freedom is birthed the day man's spirit is rekindled with the life of God, and the day his soul is rebirthed through faith in the cleansing, redemptive blood of Jesus Christ. No other definition of freedom is adequate. To gain liberty from the gravitational pull that keeps most humans earth bound, and to maintain that freedom, is the accomplishment of a lifetime. To be able to turn one's back to all the seductive calls of success, acclaim, and position is no small thing. To walk away from it all with not one backward look or regret at some point is not ordinary in any way. The greatest shackle not easily opened, and harder to escape than all others, is the fossilized lifetime image of what true "God service" really is. Jim Elliot said it exceptionally well in his statement, "He is no fool who gives what he cannot keep to gain that which he cannot lose." Life's success is all a matter of exchange. We must trade time for eternity, the earthly for the heavenly. The glamorous, temporal crowns have to be traded in on that which will not tarnish nor fade. Bible writers called it a crown of life.

We have our own view of how to serve God. Our view has been, if we serve Him in a manner that reaps for us His blessings, that is all that matters. The truth is, sinners enjoy God's blessing much the same as Christians do. To receive God's "Well done, good and faithful servant," is quite another thing. Only divine revelation breaks us free to see that having God's presence in our life is all that counts. Ultimate freedom is to live, aware 24 hours a day of the Holy, pure, life-light love of God's presence. To know of such a place is one thing, to experience it is quite another. I would have just written the book to top all books if I could now tell you that I dwell constantly in that realm I just described. I believe I can see that land of promise. I have tasted of the fruit of its full life. Nothing else draws me, even the continual flood of blessings in the natural world I live in. The law of sowing and reaping has caught up with me. If you seek first the kingdom of God and His righteousness all the things men of this world seek will be poured out upon you. So it is with me.

The thing I can testify to is that I now stand free of the tug of this life. I am free of all the things that had bound me. Power, prestige, possessions, position and plenty are no longer my prison cell guards. I am now free to pursue fully the only thing worth a human's sweat, blood, toil and tears – God for

God's sake, nothing else, just to please Him, hear Him, obey Him!

It required a two-year garage sale to rid Nathel and me of the mountain-sized accumulation of things I had collected over the years. It seemed that two or three of everything was in the large horde. Even in trying to buy a used wood stove, I gained more stuff. Thinking the stove might come in handy in a simpler life style, I made an offer. To my surprise I was told the stove was mine and everything else in the house. Several trailer loads were removed with the "stove", and added to the growing garage sale stock pile. A king sized bed, matched brace of Smith Wesson Revolvers, silverware, coin collections, Yamaha 100a 250, antiques, and bicycles, were among the items bid on by hot-eyed buyers. My cameras, projectors, and screens brought cool-eyed bargainers.

The day did come when Nathel and I stood quietly, free of house, home, and extra things, with enough money in our hands to go anywhere and do anything. That moment of immense liberty comes only once in a lifetime for a very fortunate few! People who knew my former value for nice things were sure my near miss with death from the ruptured appendix had affected the soundness of my mind. This didn't slow any of them down from rushing in to take advantage of the good deals. For me, and I speak only for myself, it was necessary to reduce my possessions, to burn the bridges and not look back. For me, and me alone, it required saying goodbye to lovely oak hall trees, carved tables, chairs, old oak crank telephones and phonographs. Things meant too much, held me too tight, the security in things up to that moment was everything. Strange and shocking as it may seem after letting go of things, I've seen my freedom, financial capacity to do and go anywhere in the world, following God's call. I agree with the statement that true divine prosperity is to have sufficient to go and do whatever is required to fulfill the true will of God for one's life.

Nathel and I did follow a special call that required leaving houses and lands, country and relatives, to begin again in a new and different way. Cashing in my school retirement was met with a major protest! Whatever will you do when you need it? "I need it now," was my answer. "I want to give it away."

The 3,000 to 4,000 dollars the retirement finally amounted to was only equal to the amount required today for a very conservative ministry trip around the world. I have spent sums equal to that retirement more than a dozen times in the last few years – with no organization, magazine, staff, or committed financial backing. I've been able to go wherever God has opened doors and said go. I've never believed in meetings for meetings' sake. A schedule has never been how the Lord has led. It isn't my purpose to tell how God provided every time, but He has! It is not a faith ministry to make an appeal letting your need be known and claim you live by faith. A faith walk is to tell God only! He alone decides who, great or small, pleases Him through their demonstration of faith. He alone decides which act of obedience pleases Him – whether one should go to be heard by thousands or be heard by only a few.

The greatest freedom in a ministry is to know that each time you go, God has sent you. I don't go because I am invited, or expected to go, I go when I have assurance and peace that God is in my going. This is freedom. I don't stay home because all the funds were not in my hand. This is freedom to be able to stay or go. To go when everything is paid in advance or to go when all is owing, is freedom. To not fret or fear or never go again is freedom. To abound or be abased, to be known or unknown and still live in great personal joy is freedom.

To have a mate, a companion, a faith partner who by faith releases you totally to serve God is freedom. Nathel told me early on when it became clear my ministry was to travel to many nations, carrying God's word of truth, hope and life, "Go and don't look back! I'll always be there when you return."

Freedom is to soar on eagle's wings to new heights of spiritual revelation, truth, and divine light; to ride on the chariots of the morning, upon the winds of God's joy, to run and not be weary, aware that champions of faith in God have run on the same path before you, to scale heights using the same handholds of the heroes of other times and generations. Freedom is to walk out full and complete obedience, combined with delight and sheer pleasure of doing so, expecting absolutely nothing in return. This is freedom.

Lift off, then steadily climb above the valley floor, at first gently, then firmly, the wind is beneath my wings and soaring has begun. It's the view of things from high above that makes the flight worthwhile.

Psalms 18:10 (KJV)

... He did fly upon the wings of the wind.

Psalms 55:6 (KJV)

... Oh that I had wings like a dove! Then would I fly away, and be at rest.

EPILOGUE

FLIGHT

Liftoff is one of life's most pleasant and truly uplifting experiences. A hang glider or ultra light aircraft may well be the ultimate in these "leaving terra firma" experiences. To "soar" free of the earth and gravity has been the dream of mankind from the beginning. My lift off experience did not include hang glider time or ultra light delight. In it, I experienced an exhilaration neither of the aforementioned thrills can compare with or provide. I can make that statement because I have made the earthly liftoffs, many times.

My first solo in a 65 h.p. Taylorcraft carried some excitement along with the accomplishment. Six hours of dual time with an instructor doesn't exactly prepare the student for all possibilities facing him on solo. It is never the solo take off that offers the challenge – it's the landing! After take off and one circuit around the airport, I was asked by my instructor to touch down.

"Stop!" he commanded, at which point he leaped out and yelled above the prop, "She's all yours. Be back in 30 minutes." The runway, once used for military training was very long. I could have made two take offs from the point where Mr. Marks, my instructor, got out. Checking for possible traffic, my eyes next scanned the relatively naked instrument panel. Oil pressure O.K., altimeter set, let's go! Pushing the throttle in smoothly brought a pleasing response from my red sky bird with its black trim. A 20 mile head wind helped provide a great take off; for just a partial moment the tail wheel left the ground and Taylorcraft and pilot sped down the runway level with earth. We didn't have much weight to get airborne. My one hundred eighty pounds plus another hundred pounds of fuel was it. Resisting the temptation to snap the responsive Taylorcraft off, I followed proven procedures. Climbing 50 feet I leveled and tipped the stubby red nose slightly earthward. Air speed indicator registered about 70 mph when I pulled the wheel back and began to climb out. I was alone at last above the earth, with only the purr of the excellent 65 H.P. engine and the cry of the wind flowing over the fuselage. Behind us the airport and terra firma receded rather quickly.

You can't get lost on a clear day in the Killetas Valley of central Washington state. To the west, the stately Cascades stood magnificently in snow capped splendor. The central Washington state university campus with its towers dominated the landscape not far from the airport. The valley was rimmed to the north by a 6000 foot ridge. To the south, canyon country opened up to receive the Kititas river. But there is an ever present phenomena always there to test the wits of any pilot, green or pro. The wind! I've learned over a lifetime of flying to respect that invisible force. The wind can do even a good pilot in.

Thirty minutes go quickly when excitement is high. Before I could believe it, my time was gone. Returning to the Ellensburg airport was much slower than my departure. Unknown to me the 20 mile wind I had enjoyed on take off was now much stronger. Arriving finally at the field, I cut diagonally into the pattern and began the downwind leg. " That sure didn't take long," I remember thinking. Still at a thousand feet elevation above the runway, I checked for carburator icing and banked into the short base leg before turning onto final. With no radio in my flying machine, I noted the green light flashed to me by the tower. My personal opinion of my base leg was that it was sloppy. It had ballooned out quite a bit. By the time I was to turn final, for some reason, I was much farther from the end of the runway than I intended to be. Normal procedure at this point in landing, the power is cut and a glide is made onto the runway. What happened found me unprepared. The moment I pulled back on the throttle, a most unusual thing occurred. The runway and as matter of fact, the complete airport seemed to back away from my Taylorcraft and me as pilot. Hum? I guess I'll have to go around and make a tighter base, I thought...must have been too wide.

Hitting the throttle, I banked right, climbed slowly to a thousand feet and made my way full length of the runway and turned left. Crossing the end of the airfield, I blasted down wind again. Ellensburg, Washington could be called Windy City. The long downslope from the Cascades invited cool air from higher elevations to roll into the valley sometimes at considerable speed. My instructor had always set a limit as to how much wind we would practice in. No discussion had ever been held as to why.

Coming quickly to base leg again, I wanted to put on the brakes. No brakes! I already had the throttle back, sure didn't need any more speed. Clearing the throttle to prevent carb icing, I glanced down in time to see the airport fire truck with several people on board heading for my end of the airport. Maybe practice, or a fire, or something, I thought. Cutting power produced the same problem I encountered on my first attempt landing. The airport simply backed away from me. By now the fire truck was at my end of the runway. Two or three men lined up on each side of the broad gray surface. There is only one thing I can do, I decided. Give her the power and fly right onto the runway! This has always been and still is called the "power on" landing. Ignorance is bliss, someone once said. I say ignorance is also dangerous. Lack of experience can also be a big time problem as well. Concerning flying an airplane at that time, my problem was both ignorance and inexperience.

Using much of the throttle and the sixty-five horse power generated by the good little engine, I managed to set down right between the two sets of men. Actually that Taylorcraft nearly hung in the air like a sea gull while the men grabbed wingstrutts on each side and pulled craft and puzzled pilot back to earth. The men hung on as we taxied slowly to tiedown, and thus complete my solo flight.

Surviving the winds that could rise suddenly in the Kititas Valley of Washington taught me much. The wind became my friend. Great updrafts would often lift my small propelled craft upward at two thousand feet a minute, saving fuel and time. A tail wind could sweep the plane and pilot along at 20 to 40 miles faster than the craft's rated 100 m.p.h top speed. I can only wonder how a bird must feel free to soar, to be carried by air currents to heights without effort. When I talk about soaring I really don't mean what one does in an aircraft or a bird on the wing. I'm talking about another kind of soaring, a kind of soaring that has no limits... where time and space do not dictate the dimensions.

At one time, my wife and I spent most of two years living in Southeast Alaska's valley by the eagles. Every year, hundreds of these magnificent creatures of the air and sky gather to feast on salmon. Salmon and eagles made a fascinating spectacle as each met at the salmon's spawning ground far from the sea. Spawning accomplished, the weary salmon were taken by the monarchs of the sky to perpetuate their life and cycle. Once I sat on a deck on a hill above Haines; three thousand feet above my head, two giant eagles were riding the strong air currents on a bright and cloudless day. My eyes watered as I tried not to blink for fear of losing view of my special prize. But, like rare things that pass from view, I simply lost sight of the grand birds above. The eagles soared out of sight lost in the vast canopy of blue beyond my straining gaze. They passed into a dimension to which mere mortals have no natural access.

So it can be, for those who penetrate the dimension in God where another kind of soaring is possible. I am not talking about some mystical out-of-the-body experience, or of levitation some claim to experience. I am talking about a flight possible only when all holds of earth, time, self, and the world about us are broken. I am talking of a time when it is possible to stand flat footed on the earth but be totally free from its power and pull. Escape into reality is but the beginning of such a flight. The ultimate flight in life doesn't happen in most lives because most individuals are intercepted and never reach the realm of such an experience.

Most people are like toddlers who break free from their parent's guiding hold and restraints to walk unsteadily off into the clasps of others and influences outside the close home circle. From day one in the wide open public school the great orientation begins. Imposing powers of teacher, books, video, and peers gradually erode, in most cases, the status of less formidable authorities called Mom and Dad. The ultimate breakaway comes subtly through the invited stranger who sits daily in the household living room. A big box encasing a giant vacuum tube brings the ultimate challenge to home influence on the school and society when TV sits uncontested as master influence in the center of the home. This star babysitter will school children in unreality and violence long before unsuspecting guardians ever become aware.

Teenage years will complete the final tutoring youth obtain in drugs, sex, and rebellion which helps them arrive at age 20 with a full load of prejudice. Most mortals will need a lifetime to unload, if they ever do, these shallow and misformed views of life. The pre-judgments of life, gained by most 20 year olds, declare that might is right and power is the ultimate. The carnage of such a concept litters the path of multitudes with broken promises, free and irresponsible sex, gain without conscience, and reward without responsibility. One can now make their way to the highest office in the land without conscience or character. Only a fortunate few are not side tracked down such a route.

For me, a gallant godly mother was able to stave off childhood acquaintances who would have led me astray. Early entrance into the church fortified Mom's value system. A fortunate friendship in my early teens with a boy of quality character served as an anchor. This friendship coupled with a next older brother's love and loyalty, served as a stabilizer, both moral and wholesome. The only way I can explain my great blessing is...God just loved me very much! Some things I can not explain however. Why did I respond to spiritual things? What was in me that held during the great temptations? No one can serve four years in the US Navy and attend a secular college for five years, and not face every temptation known to man. I was no exception, but there was one way I was different than most. I did not yield.

However, I take no credit. My explanation is that this strength within me had to be divine. I know what kept me during those formative years. There was a divine call on my life. Something in me leaned into the dealing, voice, and hand of God on my life. To have broken free of all that earth could have used to snare me, to have side-stepped the certain traps set in my path of pride, desire, and lust...only angels could have held me true. This I know for certain: something in me wanted GOD. God responded to that cry. Deep called to deep and got an answer back. God called and I responded.

Each believer's spiritual liftoff comes when they push past their own control of their life. As a junior in high school, my tremendous divine encounter with the Holy Spirit sent me speeding down God's runway for takeoff. That memorable Sunday afternoon brought the most drastic change my young life had known to that moment. My brother, Russell, had come home from a youth conference proclaiming the exciting joy of being baptized in the Holy Spirit. Russell was the most real person I know. There was no doubt in me as to the reality of his experience. I knew it was real; he was changed. That I must have my own share of this wonderful experience was my most urgent determination. The pastor, I'm sure, must have wondered what part of his sermon sent me hurrying into the prayer room after he finally finished. Actually, I waited a bit impatiently while he closed out more than an hour of preaching.

I did push past the control of my own life that day. Everything within me was emptied onto the altar of God. I was then filled with a light of such brilliance, it's not possible to describe. I had knelt in the prayer room at 1:30 P.M. that most joyful Sunday, and I came back to earth a few minutes before 6:00 P.M. that evening. That passage of time was as a few moments. I can remember speaking in a heavenly language for much of the time. I had fallen into a divine trance only to arise full of joy and able, I felt, to walk three feet above the floor. My mother and brother Russell with some other prayer warriors, as they were called, stayed with me to the wonderful climax. There was much more to me after that grand experience. A new sense of destiny gripped me. Things in my life were different, more directed. A new purpose filled me. Yes, that new destiny and direction in my life was the person of the Holy Spirit. It was He who took the controls of my life and accomplished the liftoff that caused me to soar into a vastly higher and freer realm. Now I was free from the common earthbound existence I would have known without Him.

My final escape to freedom and subsequent flight came not from breaking out of traditional prison houses and shackles forged by man. Escape for me came when I became aware of the confinements I had structured for myself. My prison guards were always the same: my self life, the draw of the world, and the myopic and temporal view of things. The flesh and the devil stood ever present outside my cell, always there to hinder and block my escape. My escape was in every way a profound miracle. God helped me break free of the gravitational pull of this world and age. The Holy Spirit cut through my chains with laser beam power. Scales fell from my eyes. I could see the light of a new day. All my values changed completely.

I have been able to soar above several major losses and disappointments. I've laid my wife and son beneath the sod. There is no measure to calculate such a loss, to measure the hurt when lifetime affiliations fracture and fade into emptiness and ashes. Shattered dreams that once stood like a crystal castle were suddenly broken and scattered before my view. Yet, out of death, loss, and disappointment, I was lifted. A powerful new and gripping vision of God's call and purpose catapulted me out of my burial ground up onto a mountain top. From that high and lofty peak of true insight and revelation, my eyes were able to look out and pierce the future. Now that I was able to see beyond the limited vista that had been my world, there came into view a new land beyond my former horizons. Divine goals and purposes now transcended my very limited former ambitions. A sunrise took place in my heart, my life, and my ministry. God and His call and purpose took over my life.

Like an eagle sensing a powerful thermal, capable of awesome upward thrust, I set my wings and took flight. Many years of the most marvelous and incredible adventures in the purpose, will, and service of God have followed. This great and grand journey has taken me around the world, to many people and countries. I have been encompassed much more than all the places, people, and things in my path. I have taken a divine journey into God.

My escape, freedom, and flight took me, in a very real sense, like an eagle up and out of sight. Many who knew me before my escape simply wondered whatever happened to the person they knew as John Clarke. There were others who explained to themselves that the loss of my wife and my own near-death experience accounted for the change in me, and the new direction my life had taken.

I'm sure it was troubling for some, to see me veer suddenly away and take another path when before I had been going wholeheartedly their same direction. Many in the church viewed me as license for their life styles. I represented the good life, good styles, and good times. Betrayal and abandonment could easily have been felt by those who had come under the power of my great dream. It was I who was leading the charge to put God on main street. "Let's take the whole country for Jesus!" was my rallying cry. What did happen? How could it be that someone like me could lose the thirst, the hunger for former things so quickly? Where did my deep need for success, acclaim, and fame vanish? The acceptable standard for these desires was clearly laid out and understood by all who attempt to climb the precarious ladder to the top. The drive for accomplishment doesn't die easily, nor is the need for recognition easily brought down to death. What a relief to no longer have the need! Free at last of the burning compulsion to have, to do, and to be, even for Jesus, vital energy still flowed, and desire, like a flame, leaped upward. Here is exactly what happened: God became my focus. The desire to be His joy, His delight, and to please Him took hold of me. Everything else fell away. It was no longer a matter of doing works for God, but to minister unto Him, to obey His voice. None of this was based on success. I no longer needed to do anything for credit. There was no longer a thrill obtained by seeing things accomplished under my hand. It's now my Lord's turn to be blessed, not mine.

I searched out how those who heard him say "Well done" qualified. Amazingly, many were unconscious of which of their acts brought their Lord pleasure. It seems their only